C000139252

INSIGHT INTO

SELF-ESTEEM

INSIGHT INTO

SELF-ESTEEM

Chris Ledger and Wendy Bray

Published 2006 by CWR, Waverley Abbey House, Waverley Lane, Farnham, Surrey GU9 8EP, UK.

Concept development, editing, design and production by CWR

Printed in Slovenia by Compass Press

ISBN-13: 978-1-85345-409-7
ISBN-10: 1-85345-409-5

WAVERLEY ABBEY
INSIGHT SERIES

The Waverley Abbey Insight Series has been developed in response to the great need to help people understand and face some key issues that many of us struggle with today. CWR's ministry spans teaching, training and publishing, and this series draws on all of these areas of ministry.

Sourced from material first presented over Insight Days by CWR at their base, Waverley Abbey House, presenters and authors have worked in close co-operation to bring this series together, offering clear insight, teaching and help on a broad range of subjects and issues. Bringing biblical understanding and godly insight, these books are written both for those who help others and those who face these issues themselves.

CONTENTS

FOREWORD

It is a privilege to write the Foreword to this short book. Self-esteem is not always named as an important topic in the range of concepts concerned with inner healing and wholeness. However, healthy self-esteem lies at the core of it all. Without it, no person functions well. The sad truth is that for most people our self-esteem suffers some serious setbacks and for all too many people it is so low that the lack of it leads to a negative and fearful approach to life. The aim of this book is to indicate how important self-esteem is, how it develops, and to offer some ways of building it up when it has been lost.

The ideas for the book began as a seminar on the subject led by Christine Ledger. Christine has faced these issues personally as a result of the long and debilitating illness of her daughter, Julia. Many a Christian parent struggles with why God does not appear to be answering prayer for family members. Christine has been there: she knows how hard it is to cope with the undermining of her self-confidence and worth, the feelings that accompany a family situation where the members for whom she has a responsibility are not 'on top' of the difficulties. I am full of admiration for how Christine has turned round her negative thoughts into seeing that God has important understanding to give to her through this painful journey. This book is the fruit of some of that learning.

The writing is illustrated with short stories of real people whose self-esteem has sunk, but is well on the road to recovery. Most readers will recognise what is described either in themselves or others known to them. We are shown how low self-esteem affects us and is accompanied by distorted images of God. Since it is the truth which sets us free (John 8:32), the book aims to challenge false or unbalanced images of God and to replace them with ones in which we can confidently place our faith. Nothing provides a firmer basis for personal healing and freedom than a strong grasp of the kindness of God towards us.

Each chapter ends with a reflective activity so that the reader can ground what has been read in their own experience. We are invited to assess our self-esteem by considering how we relate to others, how we love our bodies, how we think about ourselves and others and how we perceive God. If, then, we can face the truth about how our self-esteem has been damaged, so we can begin to listen to the caring and restoring words God says about us in the Scriptures. For just as self-esteem is greatly damaged by what parents and others say to us about ourselves, so the healing process takes hold when we believe what the only true God says about us; for it is He who ultimately matters and knows all truth.

The healing can take a long time; but the book firmly points us in the right direction.

Graham Dow
Bishop of Carlisle

INTRODUCTION

This book began its life as a seminar given by Christine Ledger at Waverley Abbey House. Its pages take their heart and soul from Christine's honest and personal approach to the problems of low self-esteem. It has merely been my job to put them in order and give them voice in another form.

The insights shared here incorporate both a foundation of established research and a wealth of practical experience. They are written for *all* of us, whether we struggle with issues of self-esteem ourselves or are seeking to help another.

As I completed the first draft of the book, I commented to Sue Wavre, senior editor at CWR, that it should be accompanied by pen, paper, a cup of tea and a good friend. We haven't been able to organise that, but I hope that my comment at least reflects well on the book's practical and God-centred content; content that will introduce those who have yet to meet Him, to Jesus – the *man* at the well.

Wendy Bray

NOTE FROM CHRISTINE LEDGER

I always enjoy being a team member working for God's glory, and the making of this book has certainly been a team effort. Wendy has so aptly taken my thoughts and words and brilliantly expressed them in written form – something I couldn't have done nearly so well myself.

We live in an age where society puts disproportionate value on those who are entrepreneurs, well-known sporting or TV personalities, and where an increasing number of magazines and TV programmes tell us to be a better parent, sibling, lover, friend and neighbour. No wonder we often find it a struggle to feel consistently 'good enough' and maintain a healthy self-esteem.

The term 'self-esteem' describes how we judge ourselves, and the value we attach to the kind of people we are. It is strongly related to the way we think a 'significant other' person in our lives sees us. These thoughts can give rise to a negative self-assessment such as: 'I'm useless; a failure; unlovable ...' We call this 'low self-esteem'. How we value ourselves may colour and contaminate many aspects of our lives and relationships, giving rise to destructive behaviour (eg addictions, eating disorders), and mental disorders such as depression. These can directly affect the way we live out our Christian lives. It is well acknowledged amongst psychiatrists and psychologists that healthy self-esteem is critical for our mental health.

For a Christian, the 'significant other' person who plays a major role in our self-evaluation is God, for it's in Him only that we will find our sense of true value and worth. Therefore, cultivating a healthy self-esteem is not about self-worship, nor about denying that we are fallen sinners – it grows from a deepening relationship with God, as we come to know Him more, in and through Jesus Christ.

CHAPTER ONE

WHAT IS SELF-ESTEEM?

INTRODUCTION

Self-esteem has become one of the most used terms in popular psychology, beloved of women's magazines, self-help tomes and tea-break quizzes.

But to allow it to remain in such a domain is to dismiss its value as one of the prerequisites of an emotionally healthy life: a life lived to the full, as God intended.

The way we feel about ourselves largely determines the way we behave and relate to other people. The level of worth or 'esteem' we ascribe to ourselves directly impacts almost every moment of our daily life and every area of it; our relationships, expectations, goals, learning styles and world-view all draw their reference points from our level of self-esteem.

WHAT DO WE MEAN BY SELF-ESTEEM?

Self-esteem draws together a number of terms which overlap in meaning: our self-image, self-concept, self-perception, self-confidence, self-acceptance, self-respect and self-worth all contribute to our self-esteem.

If you are a reader of Jane Austen, esteem will be a familiar term. It was Marianne, in *Sense and Sensibility*, who was frustrated by her sister Eleanor's proclamation of love for Edward, when Eleanor merely said she esteemed him. The phrase suited the more guarded Eleanor, because esteem denotes 'favourable regard; to regard someone with respect … as valuable'.[1]

Correspondingly, the Oxford English Dictionary defines self-esteem as 'confidence in one's own worth and abilities'. Sociologists at The University of Maryland have defined it as 'a positive or negative orientation towards oneself. An overall value of one's worth'. Alister and Joanna McGrath, writing from a Christian perspective, suggest that 'self-esteem consists of a global evaluation or judgment about personal acceptability and worthiness to be loved which carries with it pleasant or unpleasant feelings. It is strongly related to the personal views of the person by important others in his life.'[2]

Is self-esteem primarily a feeling? Or is it a judgment? Or does it involve both? The first thing to be aware of is that self-esteem is a nominalisation, a term lacking in precision, meaning different things to different people. Such diversity of definition draws different ways of understanding self-esteem to the fore.

Self-esteem ebbs and flows as we find ourselves in different situations and in relation to different people. It contributes to our understanding of the way we view ourselves; the thoughts we have about ourselves and the value we place on ourselves as people.

The qualities we assign to ourselves, whether good or bad, do not simply reflect those things we can, or cannot, do. They reflect the overall opinion we have of ourselves and the value we place on ourselves as people. The tone may be positive: 'I'm good, I'm worthwhile,' or negative: 'I'm bad, I'm useless.' A negative tone communicates low self-esteem. Healthy self-esteem is demonstrated when we can say 'I'm good, I'm worthwhile'. If someone says, 'I'm the greatest, I can conquer the world!' they would (normally!) be exhibiting abnormally high self-esteem.

So, our aim is for *healthy* self-esteem. Yet, healthy self-esteem is by no means a natural given. It is, to a large extent, a learnt behaviour

> What we live we learn. What we learn we practice. What we practice we become. What we become has consequences.
>
> > (Dr Desmond Kelly, an anxiety and depression expert)[3]

Virginia Satir, a Canadian family therapist, has written extensively on the subject of self-esteem and goes further by saying since we learn how to value ourselves, this can be unlearned; thus we can learn something new in its place. Therefore, there is hope for each one of us, that we will be able to learn how to raise our low self-esteem.

But not all of us will have access to the quality of 'teaching' we need to maintain healthy self-esteem.

Many Christians struggle with issues of self-esteem, often because of a misunderstanding about how God would have us view ourselves. Self-esteem is often confused with selfishness, and self-love with self-seeking.

Most of us will struggle with feelings of worthlessness at

times. We may question whether we are loved unconditionally and wonder whether we have any intrinsic worth. Our basic level of self-esteem will determine whether we pick up from those times, or whether they damage our self-esteem and deplete its levels further.

Healthy self-esteem means aiming for a level of self-worth and acceptance which keeps us functioning well in relation to ourselves and others, and, ideally, God; a level which enables us to reach our potential as human beings; to remain secure, able to love and be loved.

There is great value in Jennifer Minney's simple definition which says that self-esteem is 'an assurance of being lovable and loved with the ability to love in return'.[4]

SELF-ESTEEM AND RELATIONSHIPS

Self-esteem often relates to the views of significant people in our lives because we so often invest our identity in, or draw part of it from, others. If a significant other thinks that I am valuable and worthwhile, then I am. If a significant other thinks I am no good, then I believe I am no good.

We invest in a 'stock market' of self-esteem. One day our stock goes up, but on another day it goes down. If we invest a sense of our identity and esteem in others and estimate it by what they say, we can have real difficulties: their view may be neither accurate nor consistent. They may have their own investment agenda. Their own self-esteem 'portfolio' may rely on the maintenance of our low self-esteem in order to boost their own self-esteem 'returns'.

Therapists and counsellors will often have to spend time unravelling the tangle of a client's low self-esteem which has been knotted together from the inaccurate views of significant others. Gradually, clients are helped to see the reality of their dependency on those inaccuracies and to understand how those inaccuracies have adversely shaped their self-esteem.

Significant relationships are an important focal point of reference for healthy self-esteem. Both high and low self-esteem attempt to describe a psychological imbalance which occurs when we do not have our essential needs met within those relationships or within our environment. It is then that we may look for those needs to be met elsewhere.

We all have deep needs, and deeper yearnings and longings.

A helpful analogy to use is that of thirst. When we are thirsty we need to follow a chain of thought and action in order to satisfy our thirst. At first we say to ourselves, 'I'm so thirsty', but we can't press a button at the side of our head to quench that thirst. We have to identify the source of drinking water, move towards it, take a cup, and fill it with water and drink. Then our thirst is assuaged. We have to behave in a certain way to satisfy that deep longing.

At a much deeper level, we have emotional longings for a sense of:

- *security*,
- *self-worth*, and
- *significance*.

As we grow up we resemble that same cup, longing for our emotional needs to be filled. But none of us has a perfect upbringing, so although we will be 'filled up' to a certain extent, experiences, words and incidents which reduce security, self-worth or significance will drain the cup and lower our levels of self-esteem. (We will be looking at that process more closely in Chapter Two.) Low levels mean that we have a thirsting to be valued, to be longed for, and to be accepted. We will look for that source, that filling, in all manner of places and persons: often in all places and persons other than God.

We may look for it through acknowledgement of our behaviour: 'If I'm the quiet child, my teacher might accept me', even 'If I'm the rebellious teenager, my parents might notice me'. Because, when I am noticed and accepted, I will feel good about myself.

We look for it in our appearance when unconsciously we say, 'If I am slim or very beautiful, perhaps I will know fame, become a supermodel, be recognised, and my self-esteem cup will be filled because I will feel good about myself.'

We look for it in work and success: 'If I work hard and achieve, others will accept me, admire me, listen to me, and look up to me. Then I will value myself too.'

But each of these sources is short-term and shallow. They don't last and are vulnerable to drought and evaporation.

What happens if my behaviour is rejected or betrays my conscience? What if I lose my looks or illness makes me fat? Where do I go when I make mistakes at work, or someone more clever or skilled comes to take my place? What if I fail my A-levels? Will my parents still love me? Will I love myself? Our self-esteem plummets. Our cup is drained again – often to empty. All of those sources may be helpful top-ups for our self-esteem, but unless we find a genuine sense of who we are in relation to God and recognise Him as the source of our identity, we will always struggle with an emptying cup.

HOW DO WE UNDERSTAND SELF-ESTEEM FROM A PSYCHOLOGICAL VIEWPOINT?

The modern self-esteem movement was led by the American clinical psychologists William James, Alfred Adler, Abraham Maslow and Carl Rogers.

William James stated that self-esteem can be increased by achieving greater success and maintained by avoiding failures. He also thought that self-esteem could be increased by adopting less ambitious goals and through being linked to people of higher status. He suggested that what matters is whether our successes are relevant to our goals.

There is some truth in that theory, but if we start with largely unachievable and concrete goals, we will become inflexible and perfectionist. Our goals may not be achievable and we will inevitably become discouraged. Goals – even if they stretch us – must be achievable and flexible to be realistically met within the bounds of our gifts, abilities and circumstances. It's when we repeatedly fail to meet our goals that our self-esteem reduces.

Alice, an A-level drama student, has set herself a goal of winning an Oscar within four years. She believes with all her heart that she is a talented actress, and she certainly has potential. Both her youth theatre successes and her A-level tutor emphasise that talent. But Alice's goal may be better adjusted in terms of getting into drama school. When she achieves a coveted place her self-esteem will be topped up. Missing out on an Oscar before she even finishes the course would only see her self-esteem drain away with her dreams.

If our life journey is a Christian one, we may often find that God challenges us with big goals that seem beyond our abilities – that He asks us to 'step out of the boat' in faith to do something for Him. In that instance, we may need to check out our understanding of His direction with a wise friend or church leader or a 'hearing committee' who can help us listen to God and base our response and action on His biblical Word. Then, when we know He has said 'Go!' we can 'go'! There is no self-esteem booster like doing the will of the God who loves us.

We all have goals which God may choose to re-order or fit differently into His plan for our lives – some He may even do away with altogether, because He knows what is best for us.

Christine says

> I had a goal of having a family of two children, to be quite happy and everything hunky-dory, yet the reality is that I have an unwell daughter who has spent years ill in bed. My goal was shattered. Now, if that goal had been set in concrete and was one of being a mum with a 'successful' family – whatever that is – then I am not going to make it and my self-esteem will suffer. But if I think, 'This path of caring for my daughter is the one along which God now wants to take me, I can still find my value in Him, then my self-esteem is going to be much more on an even keel. I can still be a good mum in this new situation. For my goal has become flexible. I can hold on to God and say, 'I'm going to give all this to You and move towards it. If my daughter doesn't recover, I still know that You have something special for me in this situation and will work Your purposes out through my life.'

HOW DO WE UNDERSTAND SELF-ESTEEM FROM A SOCIOLOGICAL VIEWPOINT?

In contrast to James' psychological approach, Rosenberg, an American sociologist, who founded the idea of self-esteem research early in the 1960s, believed that self-esteem is more closely linked to personal qualities.

Charles Cooley, also a sociologist, connected a concept of self-esteem to our assumptions about how others view us. Cooley believed that our self-esteem is not objective in the shape of accomplishments, but is based on our anticipation of other people's appraisal of those accomplishments. So our imagination helps us see ourselves from someone else's perspective. His theory is known as the concept of the 'looking-glass self'.

Like a fairground hall of mirrors, those looking-glasses can distort the image we have of ourselves – favourably or otherwise.

As children, we grow up in a family with a certain hall of mirrors and believe 'that's how I look'. But then we enter the outside world and discover other mirrors by which to judge our reflection. Those mirrors may give a much clearer, truer reflection than the looking-glass self in the family hallway.

We are always looking for that mirror. In every encounter, environment and relationship, we are asking: 'What is my reflection?'; 'How do you see me?'; 'What am I to make of my image?' Those many images can contradict and betray one another and become distorted.

Dysfunctional parenting and family life will reflect back a distortion of that life – and family life in general – to the children, who will see themselves very differently in their parents' looking-glass. Unless someone can show them a more favourable image

– the true image – distortion will result in poor or inaccurate self-esteem.

Transformation and change begin only when we begin to believe a new 'story' that someone tells us about ourselves.

Mark was always told by his father that he would never amount to much, and that he was certainly not clever enough to become a doctor as he had hoped. His father had known long-term academic underachievement and disappointment, and constantly put down both Mark's mother and Mark in order to feel significant himself. Mark's academic ability was spotted by his teachers, who nurtured and encouraged Mark and his talent. Yet it was only once Mark had left the family home for university that he finally accepted the extent of his ability and raised his self-esteem amongst the acceptance and love of valued friends and academic colleagues. Mark was helped to recognise his worth without parental reference points because he was part of a supportive community.

Often we encourage young people to have role models, but we need to help them to make a careful distinction between inspiration and unrealistic comparison. Comparison with celebrities or sportspeople is rarely helpful. We may admire their qualities from afar, even be inspired by their achievements, but measuring ourselves against them will nearly always result in an inaccurate and damaging reflection of our own self-image.

HOW DOES LOW SELF-ESTEEM AFFECT US?

We have concluded that at the heart of our self-esteem lies the set of essential beliefs we have about ourselves: our core idea of the kind of person we are. The level of that self-esteem, whether it is deceptively high, healthy or very low, will affect our thoughts, behaviour, emotions and body state. It will impact every area of our life: work, play and relationships.

When we don't feel good about ourselves, we lack confidence. We speak negatively about ourselves: 'I'm hopeless. I'm stupid', leave ourselves out of positive circumstances, or give ourselves the least important place. That can sometimes be a kind of false humility: 'I'll sit at the back because I don't feel I'm worth very much. From there I will be able to withdraw further because I haven't much to contribute and I'll feel more comfortable.'

Most of us, even those with healthy self-esteem, will 'sit at the back' of life on occasion. But if we have low self-esteem, such behaviour goes beyond humility to damaging self-deprecation.

When we fail to recognise our significance, we lack the ability to be assertive and will become a 'doormat'. Soon we begin to resent our position and the way in which we allow others to manipulate us, to pull our strings and make us 'yes' people: people who are always afraid to say, 'No – actually I can't or don't want to do that right now.'

Our behaviour may become chameleon-like: 'I will change. Whatever colour you want me to be, I'll be that colour.' Our efforts to please all the people all the time become exhausting, our self-esteem goes down and we fail to recognise our own needs. In the extreme, we may develop a 'victim' style of personality, where we are vulnerable to bullying – even at risk of domestic violence. We may feel that who we are is in some way wrong, or that expressing our needs and wants is not acceptable. Our attitude can sabotage the good things we have in life.

Low self-esteem can present itself as a crippling fear of failure born out of perfectionism. We find it hard to cope if one tiny thing goes wrong, and consider that it negates a wider and largely positive experience. Instead of accepting a mistake, learning from it and moving on, we will wrestle with that mistake and dwell on it in an unhealthy way. We will easily feel rejected by others; believing that we do not 'match up' or that they think we are unworthy of our role.

Our sense of failure and unworthiness, often unseen by others, will draw us into a downward spiral which will drain our self-esteem.

Julia had been asked to take a greater presenting role at a conference for the charity for which she worked.

Her speaking gifts had been recognised by her employer, but she was unable to accept those gifts and worried endlessly that she was not good enough. She felt overawed by other presenters who, unknown to Julia, admired her style. Although Julia's audience would never have believed just how nervous she was, a small mistake in the detail of one presentation on the first day gave her a sleepless night. The next morning she went to her boss to say that she did not feel good enough to take part and wanted to pull out. Julia's boss was amazed and saddened. He had not noticed her mistake, and had heard only praise about Julia's performance. It took some considerable time and skill on his part for Julia to accept that she could do the job well and carry on. As her confidence increased with the warm reception she received, Julia understood that positively handling mistakes and slip-ups is part of doing things 'well'.

When our self-esteem is low we will often 'globalise' a weakness or mistake: 'Well, I'm no good at this, therefore I'm no good at anything!'; 'I failed at that, so I'll fail at the other.'

We will develop a tendency to fear the same situation when it repeats itself, and create our own self-fulfilling prophecy by 'failing yet again'.

Healthy self-esteem says, 'Yes, I failed in that. It wasn't very good, but I can learn this and do that – and improve.' We learn from the mistake, file it away in our emotional file marked 'experience', and move on. Dealing with our mistake on a 'local' scale rather than a 'global' one prevents it from becoming an area of international self-inflicted conflict!

If we cling to our failures, allowing ourselves to feel unworthy or rejected, we will develop a distorted view of ourselves, a distorted view of others and a distorted view of God.

Outcomes of long-term low self-esteem are many and varied. It is strongly implicated in depression, aiding its downward spiral into disillusion and despair.

If I feel I am not worth anything, am not loved, or will never amount to very much, my life seems no longer worth living. Self-harm may be seen as punishment and suicide as the only way forward: 'I am not worth the life I live.'

Eating disorders are also linked with issues of low self-esteem: 'If I am thin I will be acceptable, even lovable.' Likewise, teenage promiscuity and pregnancy often reflect low self-esteem as they become a search for love and acceptance.

HOW DOES INAPPOPRIATELY HIGH SELF-ESTEEM AFFECT US?

If we have excessively high self-esteem the pendulum swings in the other direction. People with high self-esteem ascribe superhuman and god-like privileges to themselves. They are unapproachable, untouchable, and often beyond reproach. The ordinary everyday rules and courtesies of life do not apply to them. They are 'above it all'.

A self-centred and inflated view of self will predictably result in a lack of concern for others, maltreatment and even cruelty. Manipulation, bribery and using other people for what are believed to be superior ends merely justify actions.

People with inappropriately high self-esteem will often become violent and abusive, especially towards those who are weak and vulnerable. They sincerely believe that they can 'beat the odds'. They are high-risk-takers, believing themselves above the law, and above just about everyone else.

Nicholas Van Hoogstraten could be said to have inappropriately high self-esteem.

Having built a property empire through the 1960s and 1970s, allegedly largely through bullying and exploitation of tenants, he has been imprisoned on numerous occasions for financial irregularities, intimidation and incitement to murder.

> He is in the process of building a £40m mansion in East Sussex at the centre of which lies a mausoleum where he says his body will be kept for 5,000 years. He is bizarrely outspoken, arrogant and frequently violent. It would appear he believes himself to be above the law.
>
> Hoogstraten is well known for his remark, 'The whole purpose of having money is to put yourself on a pedestal.'

Inappropriately high self-esteem often develops to hide damaging feelings, memories or experience – even to hide low self-esteem. But it can also be the result of psychological disorder, or of overindulgent or compensatory parenting.

High self-esteem, like low self-esteem, can be adjusted to a healthy level, but first it needs to find its true source.

WHAT DOES HEALTHY SELF-ESTEEM LOOK LIKE?

Healthy self-esteem is illustrated by a sense of balance in our lives – whatever challenges those lives contain. It is demonstrated when we acknowledge that we matter, that we are valuable, but no more or less valuable than those around us. From that secure standpoint we can give love, service and care, meet our needs and those of others and find significance in the ordinary and fulfilment in relationships.

We have healthy self-esteem when

- We take responsibility for our lives.
- We are assertive and refuse to accept bullying behaviour.
- We can say what we want and negotiate with others.

- We are able to delegate and train others to take over.
- We know how to meet others' needs, and do so.
- We are able to weather our children's rages and set firm boundaries in place.
- We are not looking for advancement, position or acclaim.
- We do not need approval or have a desire to be controlling.
- We are able to be a willing 'servant' of another.
- We are at peace with today and comfortable with ourselves 'just as I am'.
- We have good mental health.

And the ultimate source of that healthy self-esteem? The One who made us.

GOD: THE SOURCE OF HEALTHY SELF-ESTEEM

God's will for us is that we live in possession of healthy self-esteem, based on His love for us. That will is sometimes hard to accept or balance in a world where we are bombarded with alternative sources of self-esteem: money, status, beauty, celebrity, success. The world teaches that humans are the centre of the universe. That 'if it feels good – do it'. It encourages us to 'look after number one'.

Yet, God is the creator of the universe and, as such, is the source of our worth. We need to live our lives, and find our worth, according to the Maker's instructions – the Bible – and ask, 'What do those instructions for life say about me?'

God has made us with an innate sense of divine mystery. Ecclesiastes 3:11 says, 'He has made everything beautiful in its time. He has also set eternity in the hearts of men; yet they cannot fathom what God has done from beginning to end.'

If we are to discover something of the mystery of life, and live according to God's plan for eternity, it follows that the source of that life – God – is our best starting place.

By seeking Him first, discovering who we really are in God, and letting Him meet our needs, our self-esteem can be maintained at a healthy level.

God loved us so much that He made us in His image: the *Imago Dei*. That fact denotes the very relationship we have with God, a God who is in very nature, love. Steve Chalke writes that the *Imago Dei* is seen in '… our spiritual nature; our sense of moral obligation; our longing for union with God; our aspiration to goodness' and 'our desire for community.'[5] That is our starting point.

Yet that image is tarnished, distorted, broken. Our job, in encouraging healthy self-esteem, is to restore the image. We begin to do that by finding the source of our self-esteem in the God of love and grace who welcomes us with open arms.

ACTIVITY
Use 'A self-esteem scale' and the questionnaire (Appendices 1 and 2) to assess your level of self-esteem.

REFLECTION
- What does it mean to you to be made in God's image?
- How might you best use that fact as an encouragement towards a healthy level of self-esteem?
- How might you help others – friends, family, or those you counsel – to do the same?

PRAYER

Father God,

That You loved me so much that You chose to make me in Your image – with a family resemblance – is breathtaking. Help me to understand what that means for my relationship with You, my relationship with myself, and my relationship with others.

Amen.

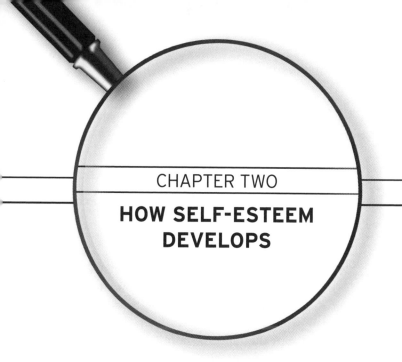

CHAPTER TWO

HOW SELF-ESTEEM DEVELOPS

INTRODUCTION

We mentioned in the last chapter that developing and maintaining healthy self-esteem depends on our ability to understand God as the source of our self-worth, and to recognise our role in restoring the image in which we are made – God's.

Our self-esteem is like an internal commentator. It commentates on good days and bad days, disastrous days and elated days. It is our job to ensure that the commentary given maintains and encourages a balanced view of our life and speaks positively into that life.

To understand the impact of the commentary metaphor, we need first to understand how our self-esteem develops, how it is strengthened and how we can maintain it as it matures and accompanies us throughout our lives.

The development and maintenance of a healthy commentary – a healthy self-esteem – depends on three areas:

- Our parents and families
- Our life experiences
- Our internal pressures: our personal standards and expectations of life.

SO ... WHERE DOES THE COMMENTARY BEGIN?

Our self-esteem utters its first words – unknown to us – at conception. Babies quickly sense whether they are wanted, loved and accepted as part of a family.

If a child is a 'happy afterthought' the initial dismay of parents may become delight and communicate itself as such. But if a child is unwanted, or is perceived to be a difficult extra burden on an already financially and emotionally stretched family, they may be only too aware of that situation: 'Well, of course my mum and dad didn't want me. I was an accident.'

There may also be issues with gender. Perhaps Mum and Dad always wanted a boy or a girl, so their child grows up feeling that they are not acceptable to their parents, simply because of their sex.

It's important to remember that none of us are the result of an *accidental* birth. We might be a surprise or ill-timed, the sixth girl instead of a longed-for boy, or stretch the finances of our earthly parents to breaking point. But God never, ever calls a birth an accident. He knew us before we came to be: He formed us and made us in our mother's womb (Psa. 139:13–16). He designed us with intricacy and intimacy. However we feel about our birth and the parenting we received, we are precious and we are His.

Our position in the family will sometimes affect how we perceive ourselves. The eldest child may be the most serious, take on the responsibility of the family and be more self-contained as a personality because they are the most senior.

A middle child may not sense any distinction in who they are – especially if they are the same sex as an older or younger child. If the youngest child, the baby, is ridiculed by their older siblings, they may gather a sense of inferiority which in itself will cause low self-esteem.

Twins Joanna and Claire were born twenty minutes apart. Joanna, born first, was the golden girl. She was tall, fair, talented, and always the centre of attention. Claire, brown-haired, quieter and small, was called 'Mouse' by her family, and her behaviour and demeanour confirmed that nickname. Timid and easily stressed, she lived in Joanna's shadow, always taking second best and putting Joanna, 'the clever twin', first.

As an adult, Claire suffered severe depression and, through counselling, was encouraged to walk out of her sister's shadow and into the light. The first task was to request that her family stop calling her 'Mouse' - at the age of twenty-eight.

Whoever said 'sticks and stones may break my bones but words will never hurt me' did not live within a family! The words that hurt us go beyond nicknames and occasional words of rebuke.

'Put downs' – words that humiliate – hurt our spirit and hurt our soul.

We can carry those messages with us for a lifetime, replaying them inside our heads, especially if they are repeated often: 'You're stupid!'; 'You're not like your brother!'; 'You're just like you're father!'; 'You're mad.' Words *do* hurt us: it is pain that calls for healing.

Barrie Wade has written a response to that oft-quoted fable:

Truth

Sticks and Stones may break my bones
But words can also hurt me.
Stones and sticks break only skin,
While words are ghosts that haunt me.

Slant and curved the words swords fall
To pierce the stick inside me
Bats and bricks may ache through bones,
But words can mortify me.

Pain from words has left its scar
On the mind and heart that's tender.
Cuts and bruises have now healed,
It's words that I remember.[1]

Words can hang over our heads like a dark shadow, almost a curse, for our whole lives unless we take steps to erase them and heal the pain.

Emotional abuse often distorts words, giving them illegitimate power. Replayed, they become like a mantra or a vow. If we are always laughed at as a child for being overweight we may say to ourselves, 'I will never be fat,' setting the scene for a lifetime of eating disorders and self-loathing. If the vow we set ourselves in response to words remains strong enough it can shape our lives: 'I'm always going to be like this'; 'I will never let them close to me.'

The words we say to ourselves will often reflect those early words of torment and teasing, and reinforce the negative beliefs we have about ourselves. We will even look for facts and experiences which reinforce those beliefs and so amplify the words.

Christine illustrates this as our tendency to have an imaginary pillar box of low self-belief: an 'I am stupid' box or an 'I'll never amount to anything' box. We will spend our lives looking for 'evidence' – things to put into the box that will confirm those views. That evidence may be in the form of experiences, statements, or yet more words. When evidence is found, we will post it in to fill the box up and confirm the status of both the evidence and the box. In doing so, we will often ignore far more important 'evidence' to the contrary, so strong is our adherence to that original low self-belief.

Yet, if we can start with a new box and ask what we would like to believe about ourselves and, more importantly, what God believes about us, we can start to fill the new box positively. With each deposit, we begin to understand that we have box-loads of God-given words – evidence to increase our self-esteem.

Hazel had always found it impossible to believe that God loved her. Her father had always been strict and distant, and she applied those same paternal traits to God. As she studied her Bible, she began to understand more of God's loving attitude towards her, but still believed His love to be distant and conditional. One morning, when feeling particularly low, she came across the verse 'Since you are precious and honoured in my sight, and because I love you ...' (Isa. 43:4). Those words reached into the core of her being as she realised the intimacy and depth of God's love, and marvelled at the beauty of the words He used to express it. Hazel copied the verse out and pondered on the idea of being 'honoured' and 'precious' and all that meant. It was a turning point in her faith and in her life: she was, at last, able to believe that she was loved by God.

Often, children will grow to adulthood with little physical closeness or affection being shown to them. They may never be cuddled or held close, never feel cherished or special. Material needs may be met – often *more* than met – but they lose value without the underpinning feeling of being securely loved.

Love is worthless without an experience of having that love demonstrated through affection, through being listened to and understood. It is meaningless without the sight of parents acting to meet needs and making ordinary parental sacrifices for their children, just because they are loved.

If children feel threatened by – or experience – abuse, whether it is emotional, physical or sexual, the damage caused goes far beneath the surface. Often, their coping mechanism will bury it. That experience may be denied for years, but it will have contributed to adult low self-esteem and will often only come to the surface, painfully, in the midst of counselling.

PERSONALITY AND SELF-ESTEEM

Of the four ancient and traditional types of personality or character – melancholic, sanguine, phlegmatic and choleric – those who are melancholic (prone to melancholy) and choleric (goal-oriented and driven) are probably more likely to have low self-esteem than those who are phlegmatic (calm and unemotional) and sanguine (optimistic, cheerful, even-tempered).

If our emotions and moods dip and rise, it is likely that our level of esteem will fall and rise accordingly, staying in step with our mood. That explains why we can often say to ourselves, 'Why do I feel so bad about myself and low today? Nothing has changed from yesterday, yet yesterday I felt so positive.' As our mood dips, so does our self-esteem.

Self-esteem may not always depend on family experience, but rather upon family characteristics or personality traits. We may 'just be made that way'. Much of our predisposition to high or low self-esteem will be genetic. It really is sometimes true that little Johnny has inherited Great Aunt Annie's blues or Uncle Jack's temper.

Wendy was amused to compare a photograph of her own daughter, then aged two, stubbornly glaring at the portrait photographer at whom she didn't want to smile, with a photograph of her mother, her daughter's grandmother, taken at the same age some sixty years earlier. It wasn't only the brown hair and cherubic-shaped face which looked the same. There was the same expression, the same stubborn lip and the same glare of fierce independence!

In the nature/nurture debate, character traits, including self-esteem levels, may be down to heredity rather than environment. Despite a healthy family ethic which prioritises praise, encouragement and valuing one another, self-doubt may still be evident in individual personalities. Two children in the same family, with the same parenting, may have markedly different levels of self-esteem. It's then that we may need to develop special interpersonal skills to counteract general low self-esteem, and remind one another of our value, especially of our value before God.

As part of a family we know each other well. We know how to push the buttons that hurt and ring the bells that help. We may need to make a conscious effort to build up rather than break down. That may mean changing the habits of half a lifetime. Because, just as low self-esteem can be learned, it can also be taught, and it is taught in the context of relationships. Sadly, people who have low esteem tend to create relationships that perpetuate it.

Lucy was referred to counselling sessions by her GP. Her low self-esteem had resulted in depression, making marriage and parenting difficult. Lucy's husband, eager to help, shared one session and drew attention to Lucy's relationship with her mother.

Lucy's mother had raised Lucy alone and had built an unhealthy co-dependency by transferring a sense of low self-esteem to Lucy, coupled with a desire that they should 'stick together' because neither would amount to very much.

Lucy admitted that she always found life harder after a visit to her mother.

She recognised that marriage and the birth of baby Josh had 'threatened' the negative togetherness she had shared with her mother, even as Lucy sought the positive togetherness that was happiness with her husband and son.

Lucy, and later her mother, began a programme of counselling, and the long and difficult process of disentangling one another from a negative past in order to build a positive relationship and a positive future.

All of us, as parents, will worry that we have damaged our children one way or another; that we haven't been a good enough parent and could have done this or that better. But whilst it is true that even if we had the opportunity to do it all again, we might not make the same mistakes, we'd be just as likely to make a whole set of different ones! We need to accept that we *do* damage our children because we are not perfect parents.

If we acknowledge that God can redeem our failings as parents, we can ask Him to do that and leave our children safely in His stronger and perfect parental hands.

We shouldn't be too hard on ourselves as parents – that alone can damage our self-esteem.

SCHOOLDAYS ... THE HAPPIEST OF YOUR LIFE?

Not for all of us!

Pause for a moment, think back to your schooldays, and recall some key moments.

It is probable that the painful experiences – the moments of humiliation, the chants or name-calling, the peer-group struggles – will be as vivid, if not more so, than any memories of sunny days spent doing handstands against the tennis court fence or kicking a football round the school yard.

The classroom and playground experience which makes up our schooldays will have given each one of us a number of scenarios in which our self-esteem takes painful centre stage.

For most of us who are now adults, school, or nursery school before it, will have been the first time that we were out in the big, bad world. There, we discovered that there is scant protection from hurtful words, no loving parent nearby to kiss our feelings better.

The very environment of school is an alien one. Huge rooms, long corridors, crowds and routines, which undermine confidence. Teachers, often unknowingly, will make comments or assumptions that start messages playing in our own solitary minds about who we are and what we can do: positive and negative. Classroom 'sets' and friendship groups mark us out as acceptable or otherwise. We all know the horror of 'picking teams' and the moment when we realise that we are likely to be the last to be picked, only to hear someone (usually sporty and popular) say, 'You can have her!'

Teasing is, in technical terms, verbal and emotional abuse. As schools adopt ever more specific anti-bullying policies it should, in most cases, be handled positively by teaching staff. But even passing comments from other pupils about glasses, the colour of our hair, the style of our shoes, can wound. For Wendy it was freckles, gangly height and long, thin fair plaits that set off the taunting. Forty years later, she can still remember how that felt.

Anti-bullying policies may now make strides to control an escalating problem, but many of us were children long before such enlightened arrangements, and still live with the scars of bullying and intimidation.

But it's not just the playground bullies who make school a threat to self-esteem. The very experience and style of learning may not be best for many of us. The timid will shrink back in a group setting, whilst the sporty will excel on the playing field, building confidence easily. Many of us will remember that it was the sporty and mathematical classmates who were popular with teachers and fellow pupils. The quieter, more reflective child, the story-writer or artist, was often left by the wayside. If that quiet reflective child was you, a glimpse of the Friends Reunited website might remind you that compared to those 'sporty and populars', you might not have done too badly at life after all!

Maddie was a quiet reflective child, an avid reader with a fertile imagination that she used to great effect to write stories and paint pictures. In the lower junior school she was taught by teachers who appreciated her gifts and encouraged her to excel, but when she joined the top junior class, everything changed. Maddie was taught by a male teacher in his sixties for whom Maths and Science ruled: words were a waste of time. He was a sarcastic bully who thought nothing of bellowing at individual children and encouraging the class to join in with his taunts. He would victimise any child who didn't see things his way on any particular day. Maddie was an easy victim. Her time in the class changed her from a quiet but contented child into a frightened and fragile one. She failed the selection exam for grammar school and underachieved all the way through secondary school because of her experience with one solitary teacher who told her she would amount to nothing. It was only when she scraped into university that she discovered that she had as much to offer as her fellow students and, through her passion for literature, finally fulfilled her potential. Maddie is now a highly respected university professor in English Literature – but she still doesn't like Maths!

OTHER CHILDHOOD EXPERIENCES

We know that any number of childhood experiences will affect our level of self-esteem. If we have experienced loss or bereavement that was not handled well by adults, either because they were absorbed by their own grief, or simply did not know how to address our needs, we will develop anxieties which affect our self-esteem: 'Did Daddy go away because he doesn't love me?'; 'Did Mummy die because I was naughty?'

Children who grow up feeling unloved because a parent leaves may have problems loving and accepting love in their adult relationships. They may even expect to be left in the same way because they feel that they don't deserve anything else.

Experiences of arguments, separation, trauma, even moving

house, can all result in self-blame: 'It's my fault'; 'If I hadn't done that …' and impact self-esteem.

As children – even as adults – we take on blame in an effort to make sense, and feel in control, of a situation that we are unable to explain. Expert counselling may be needed to help us see where the extent of our responsibility – if indeed we should take any – lies.

If we are blamed for circumstances or experiences in any relationship, we need to consider whether that blame is fair and reasonable, lest it damage our self-esteem. There is a great deal of difference between taking responsibility for our actions and living with a burden of blame that has been cast onto us by someone else who says 'It's your fault' all too often.

WHY CAN'T I?

Internal pressures, standards and expectations will vary in each of us, according to our life experience and personality type. Most crucially, they will be affected by our level of self-esteem.

If our standards are so high as to be almost unobtainable we will put ourselves forward for failure. We need to ask: 'Are these standards realistic?'; 'Are they my standards or someone else's?'

When we grow up in a family, we often take on the parent voice and internalise it so that it becomes our internal voice: the voice of standards. It hovers over us with an unspoken checklist. If we often heard our parents say, 'You tried hard', we will value our efforts. If we often heard them say, 'That's just not good enough', we will be driven towards standards which may be unrealistic and unachievable. If my parent voice says that whatever I do is never good enough, I will start believing that about myself. I may never realise that the voice is not my own, but that it actually belongs to my parents.

But if we *can* recognise the source of that voice, we can ask, 'What about me? Do I accept this? What about God? Does He accept my best? Is my best good enough for God?' And of course it is. His 'parent voice' is a voice of grace, love and acceptance and is the only parent voice worth listening to.

Most of us gain self-approval by living up to our own standards: 'I feel good when I accomplish everything on my list'; 'I need to have everything perfect in my house'; 'I feel good about myself when everyone likes me'; 'I'm OK when I don't fail at anything.' But that isn't what God says. Whilst He does set high standards for us to aim at, He leads us towards those goals with love, encouragement and understanding. He knows our weaknesses and our limitations and rejoices in what we try to do. Most of all, He looks at our hearts (1 Sam. 16:7).

Louise's mother always told her that she was 'a good little girl ... a dear little thing' and that she wouldn't be able to do the 'clever things that other people do'.

Louise was a longed-for only child whose once frail health had made her older mother overprotective. Louise's mother kept her close in order to satisfy her own need to mother and control. As a result, Louise grew up believing that she was weak and that she did not have as much to offer as other people who were stronger and cleverer than her. She accepted that she would never do the big things in life that she had always dreamt of.

Louise's mother died when Louise was in her late

twenties. Through bereavement counselling Louise began to understand that she had always listened to an internal voice – albeit loving – that was her mother's.

Louise at last found her own internal voice and, as her mother had died from cancer, decided to join a fundraising trek to Nepal. The experience changed Louise's life and she discovered gifts and capabilities she didn't know she had. Louise now works for a charity where she has been able to encourage and motivate others who, like her younger self, may feel they have nothing to offer.

THE CYCLE OF SELF-ESTEEM ...

We sometimes get to the point where, for some reason, our self-esteem is dented and we begin to believe negative messages about ourselves: 'I'm unlovable'; 'I'm stupid.' We start a cycle where one negative self-belief winds into another and forms a downward spiral: 'I'm no good'; 'Why did I think *I* could do that?'; 'I'm worthless.'

We begin to lose confidence because of the messages we are sending ourselves and begin to lose trust in other people and in the world around us: we can even lose trust in God.

We stop voicing our needs and become people-pleasers, allowing other people, who we perceive as more powerful or successful, to take advantage of us. We begin to silently resent them and wish them ill, negatively judging ourselves for entertaining such thoughts. As the cycle continues, we begin to behave in ways that are self-punitive and self-destructive and may sacrifice ourselves to them in an attempt to gain their esteem.

As a result of this continual self-abuse, and what we see as abuse by others, we find ourselves pedalling each negative thought round and round again and again: 'I am not as good as them'; 'I am useless.' (See Appendix 3.)

We need to break the cycle: to stop pedalling. Pedalling has another meaning, of course: selling our wares. Not only do we need to stop pedalling down the slope of falling self-esteem, but we also need to stop selling ourselves its wares.

THE KNOCKS OF ADULT LIFE

Even if we have had a wonderful childhood, carefree schooldays and spot-free teenage years, there will often be experiences in adult life that severely dent our self-esteem.

The everyday grind of life can sometimes resemble a tough survival course. We may feel taken for granted by family and know little appreciation for a job well done at work.

Our kindness may be misinterpreted by neighbours, we may feel forgotten or rejected by friends or live with constant put-downs by partners – perhaps because their own self-esteem is low. We may be unfairly criticised or wrongly accused, deceived or betrayed by someone in whom we place our trust.

In our church fellowships, we may not know opportunities to use our strengths and gifts or fulfil our potential for taking responsibility. It is often in the context of church, the very place where we should feel safe and nurtured within a community of love and acceptance, that we are hurt most. We often feel battered and bruised as our experience destroys our faith in people, and stretches – even snaps – our faith in God.

There is some irony in the fact that the Church is a communion of saints: it doesn't always feel that way!

We need to remind ourselves that we are all fallen human beings who God accepts and loves in that very state. Often we are the ones who need to take responsibility for our own reactions and responses. Before we think our friend is rejecting us, we need to ask: 'Did she pass by on the other side of the road and ignore me? Or has she lost her contact lenses?' If we feel that we are considered useless in any form of ministry we need to ask: 'Did the minister intentionally ignore my offer of help with the meeting? Or did the message containing my offer of help not get through?'

The details of day-to-day church living need grace and forgiveness and huge amounts of benefit of the doubt if we are not to allow them to chip away at our self-esteem and inevitably make us a whole lot more prickly, sensitive and unapproachable in the process.

However much we are prepared to take responsibility for our response, and however much we learn to forgive and forget, there will still be difficult times inside and outside church life. Whatever happens, we need to hang on to the assurance that 'I know who I am in God'.

THE DISAPPOINTMENTS OF FAITH

Prayers that are apparently unanswered – or not answered in the way we would like them to be – will inevitably make us think 'God doesn't care; God has forgotten me.'

Faith and self-esteem take a downward drop together. We begin to think of all the things that aren't quite right about life and hook our unanswered prayers onto them, asking endless questions of God, forgetting what faith is really all about. We forget that faith is trust, and trust – to coin a teenage phrase –

'whatever' happens.

In one of his songs, *For this I have Jesus*, Graham Kendrick refers to prayers that as yet seem unanswered. If you know the song, you will know that its context is the assurance that in all the mysteries and disappointments of faith, we still have Jesus. However we might feel, whatever we might see to the contrary, we can be assured that He knows our situation, that He does care and that He never forgets us.

Christine tells the story of God's very practical intervention at a low point in her life

> My daughter is still ill, but was very, very ill for about ten years with ME, spending most of her time in bed. In order to have a bath she would crawl out to the bathroom, have a bath, then lie on our bathroom floor for the next hour to recover any energy to crawl back to bed again. She couldn't read and wasn't well enough to have visitors.
>
> We would sit round her bed, read Bible verses and pray. On some days she was not even well enough to eat her food, devoid of all energy, and struggled with high temperatures and swollen glands.
>
> I was at a very low place. I distinctly remember ironing in the kitchen and thinking, 'Well, Lord, as You haven't answered my prayer, I must have done something wrong. I'm of no value, otherwise you would have answered our prayer and the prayer of so many who are praying.' But I caught myself and said, 'No, Christine, don't go down that route because that way is the way of lies.' I had to be determined to get hold of myself and say, 'You're not going to accept that!' But it was very hard. My faith was battered, my self-esteem was battered. I was worn out with trying to stay with, where and who I was in God. I was hanging on – just – but I still felt forgotten by God.

Then my daughter had a visit from one of her friends. After she had spent time with my daughter, she came downstairs for lunch, and said, 'Christine, I want you to know that God says He hasn't forgotten you. God has told me to come and look after your daughter and take her away to the flat so that you and your husband can have three months' break.'

God was there; He had answered my prayer and intervened. I was not forgotten. That young woman's obedience had carried His care to us all.

We will probably all go through wilderness experiences at some time or another or experience a 'dark night of the soul'. Lost and lonely we will cry out, 'Where are you, Lord?'

Of course, those experiences are largely based on our feelings. We are a feeling people. We will *feel* abandoned by Him, just as if He is not there.

Yet, strangely, the Bible is full of accounts of people meeting God in the midst of their desert experiences. Not before a great deal of isolation, anguish or uncertainty, but meeting Him nonetheless, often at the very lowest moments. Then they come face to face with the certainty of who God really is.

God's love and His faithfulness are not feelings, they are certainties; facts.

The fact that we don't feel His presence does not deny the fact of its reality.

ACTIVITY
Spend some time reflecting on your own self-esteem 'history'.

CHILDHOOD
Was my self-esteem as a child affected by:

Family experiences and relationships?

_____

Losses and trauma?

_____

School?

_____

MY OWN INTERNAL PRESSURE
- How and why do my standards affect my self-esteem?
- Are my standards realistic? Yes . . . . No . . . . Sometimes
- Are they my standards or do they belong to someone else?
- Do my internal standards run my life or am I in charge of them?

Most of us gain self-approval by living up to our own standards:

'I feel good when I accomplish everything on my list.'
'I need to have everything perfect in my house.'
'I feel good about myself when everyone likes me.'
'I'm OK when I don't fail at anything.'

List four standards you have for your life. Describe how these relate to your self-esteem:

1 _____
2 _____
3 _____
4 _____

Ask yourself:

- Which adult experiences have dented my self-esteem?

- How do I reflect on those experiences now?

- What might I do about my self-esteem history in the light of what I have read?

REFLECTION
- Read Zephaniah 3:17: 'The LORD your God is with you, he is mighty to save. He will take great delight in you, he will quiet you with his love, he will rejoice over you with singing.'
- Spend a few moments reflecting on that image of God comforting you with His own lullaby ...
- What does that image tell you about how God loves you?
- How does it measure your worth?
- How does it challenge the feelings you might have in the dark times that suggest God has forgotten you?

PRAYER

Father God,

Remind me that the only 'internal' voice worth listening to is Yours; that You are 'mighty to save' me from a lifetime cycle of low self-esteem. Help me to lay my life before You in prayer so that You can delight in me, rejoice over me with singing, and restore me to my rightful place as Your much loved child.

Amen.

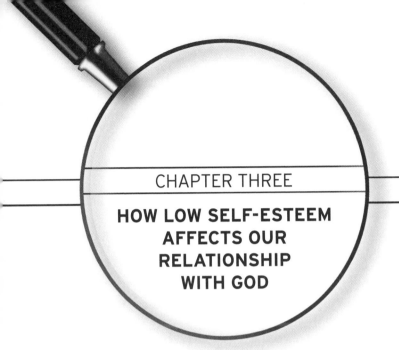

CHAPTER THREE

HOW LOW SELF-ESTEEM AFFECTS OUR RELATIONSHIP WITH GOD

INTRODUCTION

For Christians, healthy self-esteem means having the right image of God.

God is not only the source of life – He is the source of our identity. We are made in His image. Having a distorted image of God will result in us having a distorted image of ourselves. Conversely, having a distorted image of ourselves will result in a distorted image of God. It's the 'catch-22' of image and identity. How do we release ourselves from its grip?

HOW LOW SELF-ESTEEM GIVES A DISTORTED IMAGE OF GOD

Most of us developed our concepts and feelings about our heavenly Father from our earthly mothers and fathers, and these feelings become intertwined and confused. But the guilty and contradictory feelings are not the voice of God. They are often the continuing voice of Mother or Dad or Brother or Sister, or something internalised that puts pressure on us.[1]

Here are the echoes of the very powerful voices from the past we spoke about in Chapter Two. An example of the fact that 'We don't see things as *they* are ... we see them as *we* are' (Anais Nin).[2]

Our image, or images, of God – because sometimes we have many – are critically important to our spiritual well-being. If we have a distortion of who God is, we will not have a healthy estimate of ourselves as people.

Our image of God will usually influence us more powerfully than our ideas of doctrine, or any statements we hear made about God, because personal images are rooted in powerful emotional experiences. Our images of God affect both how we feel about God and how we behave in response to His Word. We are on a lifelong quest to find and accept a true image of God.

The replacement of distorted images of God with biblically accurate ones isn't an easy process, but it is a continuing one. We are all in the ongoing process of replacing our distortions with truth, of restoring the image of God in our lives.

From a scientific point of view, the images that we have and the thoughts about those images have created pathways in our brain. What we are trying to do is create new images and make new pathways – and that takes time.

A winter driving analogy helps us to understand that process. If we are driving down a familiar hill across a thick blanket made by a heavy fall of snow, our car tyres automatically sink down into the ruts that have already been made. It's the comfortable, predictable way to go. To get out of those ruts for good is difficult, because we skid back into them again. It is not unusual, in snow- or sand-bound countries, to read roadside signs that warn: 'Choose your rut carefully – you'll be in it for 200 miles!'

In the same way, we need to get out of our predictable tracks of thinking, challenge and question the distorted images we have of God, and replace them with a clear and true image. Even if that means – and excuse the mix of metaphors – etching them again line by line. We need to do that because often those distorted images of God actually affect our low self-esteem, which affects our distorted image of God and consequently our relationship with Him: another negative cycle. An accurate image of God will increase our self-esteem and help us develop a good relationship with God. When we have a good relationship with God our self-image becomes more accurate and that increases our self-esteem: a positive cycle.

DISTORTED IMAGES OF THE FATHER

Some of us may struggle with our relationship with God the Father, more than with the Son or the Holy Spirit, largely because we have had difficulties with fathers – or father figures – in our own human relationships.

The distorted images we have of God as Father fall into six main areas:

- Seeing God as the father of impossible expectations;
- Seeing God as the father who abandons;
- Seeing God as the abusive father;
- Seeing God as the emotionally distant father;
- Seeing God as the unreliable father;
- Seeing God as the disinterested father.

SEEING GOD AS THE FATHER OF IMPOSSIBLE EXPECTATIONS

Children have a deep need for approval from their parents. If, as children, we don't *feel* that approval we develop and replay negative messages, not only about ourselves but also – perhaps later – about God, our heavenly Father.

As a result, we see God as one who is never pleased with us. His standards seem unachievable and His expectations unattainable.

Bible verses which remind us of God's command to be obedient may cause guilt to arise: 'I'm not a good enough Christian, am I? God the Father is asking me to do this and I can't do it and therefore I'm an awful Christian.' Straightaway, we're on that cycle of self-esteem again, pedalling away from the Father who loves us.

We may also have difficulty believing those verses which proclaim God's unconditional love. The barrier is a very real one, because it is not about head knowledge – 'You must know that God loves you!' – but about needing to *experience* what it is to be loved and accepted unconditionally in a human relationship, in order to feel loved unconditionally by God.

Such needs highlight the necessity for us, as Christians,

to love one another unconditionally: to do so both in family relationships, and within a church family. That's why effective and loving pastoring in the church is key to building the self-esteem of those who are pastored.

David Seamands in his book, *Healing for Damaged Emotions,* vividly describes such an image of God

> God ... is seen as a figure on top of a tall ladder. [The person] says to himself, 'I'm going to climb up to God now. I'm his child, and I want to please Him, more than I want anything else.' So he starts climbing, rung by rung, working so hard until his knuckles are bleeding and his shins are bruised. Finally he reaches the top, only to find that his God has moved up three rungs, so he puts on his Avis button and determines to try a little harder.
>
> He climbs and struggles, but when he gets up there his God has gone up another three rungs ... God is that little inner voice that always says, 'That's not quite good enough.'[3]

If we see God as the God of impossible expectations we will tend to think that way. We will feel that God is never satisfied; that we can never do enough. We continually strive to please God, yet never feel that we have pleased Him – our self-esteem tumbles down the ladder.

We need to bring the right and biblical image of God into our thought processes: God as a gracious and merciful Father who delights in His children. He has compassion on all He has made (Psa. 145:9) and has created us for His pleasure (Psa. 149:4; Rev. 4:11). He accepts us totally, exactly as we are.

ACTIVITY/REFLECTION

Read Psalm 145
- What does this psalm teach you about God's character?
- Identify the qualities or actions of God which speak to you personally.
- What does it say about God's expectations of you?
- How does this biblical image of God help you to believe and feel more acceptable and loved?

SEEING GOD AS THE FATHER WHO ABANDONS

Children or teenagers who experience divorce, separation, death or prolonged absence of a parent will struggle to a greater or lesser degree. Separation may not always be as a result of parental relationship breakdown, rather an occupational hazard. It may be that a father works away – perhaps in the Forces or on an oil field. A child may not always understand that absence, even when the reasons are consistently explained and demonstrated.

Some years ago, Wendy taught a number of children from an air force base whose fathers all belonged to the same squadron. When that squadron left for exercises the emotional instability of the children was evident and marked, even in a classroom situation. There was a heightened level of personal anxiety and an increased incidence of classroom relationship problems which could be traced back to feelings of insecurity and low self-worth. Children made higher demands of one another in terms of loyalty and often accused friends of excluding them or ignoring them. Once the squadron returned, relationships improved and the children were much happier. Especially if Dad had returned bearing gifts!

If a child believes that the parental absence is their 'fault', self-esteem goes down. Anxiety may suppress self-esteem as they consider, 'Well, what if my dad leaves again. How will I cope?' The 'what ifs' that feed anxiety can starve self-esteem and prevent its healthy growth.

When young people have experienced abandonment, they often take on the overall responsibility for the family: 'I must be responsible for keeping everyone happy then they won't leave me.' A finalist in the TV series *The Apprentice* admitted that her early life experience of loss and abandonment had been pivotal in driving her to achieve in business, in order to provide for her younger siblings and to keep the family together.

As young people who have known loss and abandonment embark on a relationship with God, or consider His involvement in their life, their questions and expectations will be similar: 'What about God? Will He abandon me? What must I do to make sure He will keep on loving me?' It becomes difficult for a young person with an experience of abandonment to know and experience that God is faithful. It will be equally difficult for them to accept that God is a father who will never leave them or forsake them. Their fear of abandonment by a heavenly Father is logical and real.

The biblical image is very different. God the Father says, 'Never will I leave you, never will I forsake you' (Heb. 13:5).

The image to be restored is the image of a father who *stays*.

Cathy took some time to accept that God would not desert her when things went wrong in her life. Unable to face the responsibility of caring for his family, Cathy's father had often left the family home for several weeks when life became tough – most notably after redundancy, during financial crisis and when Cathy's mother had a miscarriage. Cathy's image of God was of a loving but weak father who could not be relied upon to always be around.

Consequently Cathy developed a tendency to 'leave God out' of her crises, believing He would not be there for her.

ACTIVITY/REFLECTION

Reflect on a time when you felt very alone, abandoned or forgotten.

Read John 14

- Jesus had told His disciples that He was about to leave them (John 13:33). He recognised that their emotional reaction to the loss of His presence would be like a child's pain at the loss of a parent. Hence He uses the image of 'orphans'.
- Does that image relate to you in any way?
- How does Jesus comfort His disciples?
- What gift did Jesus promise them (John 14:16–17)? Have you received this gift?
- What future did Jesus promise His disciples? Are you able to relate positively to the image of the 'Father's house' with 'many rooms'?

SEEING GOD AS THE ABUSIVE FATHER

God put children in families so that their need for affection and approval could be met by loving parents who would build them up with encouragement and love. Sadly, too many children hear harsh words instead of loving approval and know indiscriminate physical punishment rather than tender affection. They live in an unpredictable environment where they can never be sure of the responses of their parents: a climate of fear and insecurity.

A logical consequence is that in coming to faith they will view a heavenly Father as equally harsh, controlling, demanding and easily angered. They will perceive God as 'Dad with a big stick', issuing demands and handing out punishments with inconsistency and without mercy or grace.

If children have been sexually abused they will grow up to feel suspicious and guilty – even if that guilt is buried – and will have difficulty feeling forgiven and clean before a Father God who loves them. They will refuse to accept that they are accepted and loved unconditionally, or may be unable to trust the motives of a heavenly Father. For some adults seeking faith, just the word 'father' can set a very real psychological barrier in place that may take years of counselling and prayer to remove so that healing can be known. They will just not feel able to trust that aspect of God's character.

Yet the Bible tells us repeatedly that God can be trusted, that He is a God of love and faithfulness, of forgiveness and grace. He is 'slow to anger' (Psa. 145:8). He doesn't throw hurtful words at us, or leave us feeling guilty and ashamed. His discipline is gentle and loving and for our own benefit rather than for the expression of His anger. He is the Father of compassion (2 Cor. 1:3) and the God of all comfort, the One who heals our brokenness.

Those who have known abuse from their father, or from other adults in authority, may require expert counselling and care from specialist Christian agencies – and much prayer.

Tom had an abusive relationship with his father, who swung from being emotionally distant to very aggressive. He made unreasonable demands on Tom, often depriving him of meals and school necessities as punishment. Tom's greatest problem was his battle with a tendency to replicate similar, if less severe, behaviour with his own children. Tom was mentored by a wise older man in his church and through counselling, prayer and Bible study, gently learnt about God's fathering – and consequently how he should father his own children.

ACTIVITY/REFLECTION

What personal experiences might have affected your ability to believe that your heavenly Father wants to bless you, rather than hurt you?

Look at the following images of God and reflect on the one that is the most meaningful for you. Consider writing a personal psalm incorporating your thoughts.

- Comforter (Jer. 8:18)
- Father of compassion (2 Cor. 1:3)
- Father to the fatherless (Psa. 68:5)
- Refuge (Psa. 9:9)
- Deliverer (Psa. 18:2)

SEEING GOD AS THE EMOTIONALLY DISTANT FATHER

It is important that as children grow they know that they are heard and that their feelings are validated and acknowledged. If children are not helped to understand their feelings, they may become ashamed of those feelings and their self-esteem will be damaged.

Parents may dismiss or minimise the feelings their child wants to express: 'Big boys don't cry!'; 'Don't be silly!'; 'You shouldn't feel like that.' As a child we feel powerless to communicate our vulnerabilities and our hearts cry out, 'But this is how I feel!'

How we deal with our feelings as children will set the scene for adult life. If we have used demanding tactics in order to be heard as children, whining and tantrums, ultimatums and emotional blackmail, we will be very likely to use those same tactics in adult life, manipulating those we love to meet our demands – even God. We may need to relearn how to communicate our feelings and emotions in a healthy way that gives space for us to be heard, but that also requests that we allow the emotions of others to be heard.

Feelings are neither right nor wrong: they are as unpredictable as the weather. If we perceive that people, parents or otherwise, can't cope with our feelings, we keep them hidden. Negative feelings left unspoken can lead to guilt, anger and fear. Yet, as Christians we should encourage one another to validate emotions, to listen to them rather than deny them under a banner of platitudes.

A loving, sharing, sacrificial church is one which accepts us, gives us a safe place to share our emotions, and says that it's OK to feel and to share with honesty.

God is not an emotionally distant father. He is accepting – even encouraging – of our emotions. We sometimes forget that God is an emotional God. The Bible tells us that He laughs, cries, shows patience and sometimes loses it, forgives, forgets, remembers and understands. He feels jealousy and rage, tenderness and affection and deep, devoted, abiding love.

As we are made in His image, our emotions will reflect His emotions – emotions He designed. Because of that mirroring, He understands our emotions. It is only in close relationship with God that we will also learn to understand those emotions. The Psalms with all their honesty and anger, desperation and reconciliation illustrate that fact vividly.

Jayne shared with an elder at her church that she was unable to pray about feelings, only about facts and material needs. She was helped to recognise that her tears had embarrassed her father as a child and that she had consequently hidden her vulnerable self behind a list of material and intellectual needs which her father felt more comfortable with. Jayne was helped to discover that her God was an emotional God and that her emotions - and her honest expression of them - mattered to Him.

ACTIVITY/REFLECTION
What past experiences may have affected your ability to know that God is emotionally close and approachable?

Read Hebrews 4:14-16

- Jesus is able to 'sympathise with our weaknesses'. What does this say to you?
- As you face current trials and struggles, what difference does it make to know that God cares about you emotionally?

SEEING GOD AS THE UNRELIABLE FATHER

Children need to experience a love which is reliable and predictable. As they grow it is important that at least one significant adult in their life is absolutely reliable and consistent. If that significant adult cannot be relied upon – is always late picking them up from school, breaking promises or going back on their word – a child begins to live with a sense of insecurity. He or she will become anxious and unsure of what might happen next and feel increasingly insecure: insecurity damages self-esteem.

With such children, unreliability will gradually become the norm in expectations of others because expecting consistency will only have led to disappointment. They may even recognise that they cannot change their parent in order to know security. They become disappointed, disillusioned, give up and decide they can't trust other people. Consequently, they believe that they can only rely on themselves, becoming self-sufficient and self-motivated – often to an unhealthy extent. Not only will they see God as unreliable, but they will find it hard to trust Him and to learn to lean on Him.

In conclusion, they will say 'I can't rely on God. He makes promises He may not keep'; 'Why doesn't He answer my prayers?'; 'Can I be sure He will keep His promises?'; 'How do I know He will listen to me?'; 'He says this but I don't believe Him.' Those questions of faith are hard enough when we have learnt to trust God, but if we don't know what it is to trust and have our trust rewarded by adults in our own lives, those questions become more painful and complex and may further reduce an already low level of self-esteem.

Each of us has to learn to trust God step by step. Those steps are more gradual if we have not learnt to trust person to person. It may take a very long time for those who have been unable to trust in relationships to learn to trust God: to not just *understand* that He can be trusted as fact, but to *experience* God as a reliable father.

God knows the difficulties trusting involves for many of us. If we sincerely want to learn to trust Him, He will help us to do so.

Margaret needed constant reassurance from her church leader that he would keep his word in a pastoral care situation. Her church leader recognised that this was as much of a problem as the pastoral situation itself and encouraged Margaret to voice her anxieties.

Margaret recognised that she had never been able to rely on her adored father who had been divorced from her mother when Margaret was six. He would always make excuses for missed visits and trips out, and on one occasion Margaret had seen him in a nearby town with a woman when he had told her he was too ill to take her swimming. Her inability to trust and believe assurances had stemmed from her experiences with her father and had extended itself not only to other adults in authority - like her church leader - but to God too.

ACTIVITY/REFLECTION

Which of your early childhood experiences may have led you to believe that people are either reliable or unreliable? How did you feel when someone let you down?

Read Psalm 36:5–12
- How is God described?
- Which words suggest that God is faithful and reliable?
- Which image of God do you find the most helpful?
- What difference would it make if you had a deeper faith in a God who is utterly faithful and reliable?

SEEING GOD AS THE DISINTERESTED FATHER

Children need to feel valued as an interesting person in their own right. When a parent shows an interest in a child, their sense of self-worth goes up. Inevitably, busy lives mean that parents don't always give time to their children, or may, knowingly or unknowingly, limit that interest to what their child *does*, rather than in who their child *is*.

If a child's experience of life is one in which people rarely, if ever, listen to what they have to say, or show any interest in them, they will begin to think, 'I'm not worthwhile as a person'; 'People are not interested in me, they don't listen to me'; 'How can I be of value?'; 'They don't really take me seriously.'

If Dad has 'a big important job' to do, and doesn't have time for me, I will feel less important. But if Dad involves me in his 'big important job' in some way, sharing his day, letting me sit at his desk, I will feel important as part of that job – even when I know he is busy.

67

Those who have experienced their parents as disinterested often project that expectation upon God, believing that He will have little interest in them.

It follows that where God is concerned – a big, important God with a big important job to do – God the Father is not interested either.

In adulthood, such a distorted image may lead to a belief that 'I can't pray for myself. I can pray for everybody else, but I can't pray for myself because I am not important enough/God is not interested in me.' The expectation of God is low, reflecting a sense of low self-worth.

But God is interested in the very tiniest details of our lives. He gives us a myriad of images in the Bible where He shows us that He is interested. Interested as a counsellor (Isa. 9:6); as a nurturing mother eagle (Deut. 32:10–11); as spouse (Hosea 2:16); even as hairdresser (Luke 12:7)!

What's more, God wants us to be part of His plan, part of His 'big important job'. He wants us to be involved in it, using our gifts and abilities. We *can* 'sit at His desk' and share in His work. He believes that we are that important to His work – so shouldn't we believe that too?

This sharing of His work isn't about what we can *do*, but about who we *are*: loved children of a busy but involved Father, a Father who always has time for us.

There is nothing we can do to make God love us more and nothing that we might do that will make Him love us less.

God is not just interested in us – we fascinate Him!

Both of Julie's professional parents worked long hours, having little time for her. As Julie studied for A-levels, they simply told her to apply for 'the best universities'. Julie was understandably anxious but she did not, at first, seek God's guidance, or ask her youth Bible study group to help her pray through her choices. She believed that it was down to her and that God could not possibly be interested in the shape of her future.

Her friends from the study group told her about the experiences of other students and the way in which God had attended to even the smallest details of their university applications. Julie was encouraged to pray through the process as she applied and, as a result, was given a greater sense of security in her choice – more importantly, she gained the revelation that God cared about the details of her life.

ACTIVITY/REFLECTION

How hard is it for you to know that a loving Father God listens to you? What past experiences affect your knowledge that you are of infinite worth to God?

Choose one of these images of God and reflect on one of the pictures of a father who is attentive and interested in you. In response, write a letter to God.

- Counsellor (Isa. 9:6)
- Mother eagle (Deut. 32:10–11)

- Spouse (Hosea 2:16)
- God with us (Matt. 1:23)
- Helper (Heb. 13:6)

Perhaps the most important thing we can do to build our own self-esteem is to understand and know God. In the context of our relationship with Him we will develop a true and clear image of God, which will help us discover a true and clear image of ourselves and a healthy level of self-worth and self-esteem.

We are made in God's image and it is in God that we find our true identity and worth, as we delight in Him and He in us!

> As I gaze into your eyes
> Such a look of pure delight I see
> Lord, you're smiling at me![4]

ACTIVITY
Write 'Made in His Image' on a piece of card or paper and place it above a mirror you use each day.

REFLECTION
- Look over the notes you have made from this chapter; remind yourself of the formation of your identity in God.
- Think about the way in which your relationship with Him helps you feel secure in that identity.

Remind yourself that:
God
… accepts me as I am
… is always with me
… listens to me
… is gentle and tender
… understands my emotions
… is fascinated by me!

PRAYER

Bring yourself before God, just as you are, and turn your thoughts into prayer.

CHAPTER FOUR

IMPROVING SELF-ESTEEM

INTRODUCTION

So, how do we improve levels of self-esteem, both in ourselves and in others? By writing a new 'story of self' that takes in every chapter of who we are, from God's perspective. We begin to do that by acknowledging what makes us who we are – our many selves – and how those elements affect our self-esteem: our thinking self; our behavioural self; our physical self; our emotional self and our spiritual self.

SELF-ESTEEM - THE THINKING SELF

It was Descartes who said, 'I think, therefore I am.' We could argue that the Bible teaches the opposite: 'I am, therefore I think', because God first created Adam with a sense of curiosity. So, as the first human 'I am', Adam was created.

But, as we know, his sense of curiosity and his ability to think and reason actually got him into trouble. His very thinking, about his existence and his choices, meant that he abused those choices when he shared the forbidden fruit with Eve.

So perhaps we could rightly link the two statements and say, 'I am, therefore I think. I think, therefore I am.'

Our awareness of the way we think is very important to our self-esteem. Every thought gives shape to our attitudes and decisions: 'Be careful how you think; your life is shaped by your thoughts' (Prov. 4:23, GNB).

Although we talk to each other at the rate of about 500 words a minute, researchers say that our internal thoughts, what we say to ourselves, can sometimes rattle away at 1,500 words a minute. If the majority of those thoughts are negative we are loading up a considerable amount of ammunition with which to shoot holes in our self-esteem.

If we could tape our thought patterns for one twenty-four hour period, we would probably be shocked. Not just at the petty criticism and moaning, the themes we dwell on and the attitudes we take, but at the very negative patterns we think by. We can help ourselves and others who are challenged by low self-esteem through listening to thought patterns. The clearest way to do that is to listen to what is actually *said*. Our aim will then be to challenge and change those negative patterns for the better to transform our thinking.

We are reminded in Romans 12:2 to '…be transformed by the renewing of your mind' (see Appendix 4). Notice that this verse does not suggest that we will be renewed in our thinking instantly. Rather, it implies that the renewal process is an ongoing one. Renewing our thinking, including transforming our negative thinking into positive thinking, is something we have to work on constantly, on a daily, hourly, minute-by-minute basis. Sometimes, just a moment of negative thinking can sink a week of positive thinking. The more we engage in negative thinking, the more our thoughts will affect us emotionally.

So what constitutes negative thinking?

When we are listening to ourselves and others we will be able to pick out negative thinking patterns, through clear indicators:

- 'Shoulds' and 'oughts' ... put a demand on oneself and others, and this drivenness causes frustation and guilt.
- 'I'm this' or 'that' can be indicative of negative self-labelling.
- 'I never', 'I don't' can be an indication of believing a negative self-fulfilling prophecy.
- 'I'm no good' or 'I'm useless' is a sign of putting myself down.
- 'He/she said' indicates hearing others' commentaries, true or otherwise, about us.

Of course, in someone with healthy or exaggerated self-esteem, those phrases would be framed positively or used in the extreme. But as we listen to someone with low self-esteem we will notice a negative string of thoughts which confirm one another and link together to pull self-esteem downwards.

These phrases contain uncomfortable words indicating uncomfortable feelings. It's important for us to acknowledge the negative thoughts that are attached to our uncomfortable emotions, not just to cover them with the sticking plaster of 'look on the bright side' responses.

If we acknowledge those thoughts, we can then choose to

challenge them effectively. It's as if we take our negative thoughts to court and put them in the dock. We look at the evidence they give in their defence – our supposed guilt for example – and ask whether we really *are* to blame. We question the thoughts and weigh the evidence to get to the truth. When we find the evidence unfounded we say, 'I'm not to blame for this. Not guilty', and throw the negative thoughts out of court.

In place of the dubious, inaccurate evidence and the negative thoughts we have thrown out, we can look for the true and positive words that God speaks about us and choose to agree with them.

Marjorie was in her late sixties and had enjoyed a close and happy marriage.

Yet after her husband's death she suffered complicated grief compounded by guilt. Marjorie had always said to her husband, 'When you die, I'll be with you.' When her husband collapsed in the garden with a heart attack, he said 'Do stay with me.' Marjorie agreed, 'Of course I will!' Understandably, she needed to first run indoors to call the ambulance. When she joined him again in the garden he was falling unconscious. Marjorie felt that she was to blame, and that if she had not left her husband he would not have deteriorated. Sadly, he died soon afterwards.

In counselling, Marjorie was helped to understand that she had done what was necessary in the circumstances and had given him the very best of care. If she hadn't called for an ambulance there may not have been any hope in the situation. Although her husband had died she was helped

> to understand that 'I did what I could' and her guilt was able to be resolved.

There *will* be times when our guilt is genuine guilt rather than false or assumed guilt. Then it is important to take responsibility for our wrongdoing or weakness, confess the sin and ask Jesus to replace that guilt with His forgiveness and truth. Only then can we be free from the burden of guilt as we hang on to His assurances that we are forgiven and 'free indeed'.

For someone without faith, such a process might involve the self-examination of guilt in order to take responsibility for actions, to ask forgiveness of another – even of themselves – and find some resolution. If we are helping them, we may need to ask, 'What does forgiveness mean to you?' If their ideas are distorted or confused or they find the concept of forgiveness difficult to understand, we might present a Christian framework for forgiveness as a 'healthy' framework for them to work with. In practical terms, they may consider who they need to seek forgiveness from – themselves or another person – and what that would mean to them.

Forgiveness does not require the person who has been wronged to forget or condone what has been done to them, but it does require enormous courage.

Forgiveness is never easy. M. Scott Peck, in *The Lost Art of Forgiving*, calls it 'the agony of forgiveness'.[1]

But we are called to forgive 'just as in Christ God forgave [us]' (Eph. 4:32)

Negative thought patterns can lead to a more entrenched

attitude about our own tendencies: negative bias. A negative bias means that I will always blame myself when things go wrong, whoever or whatever – if anything or anyone – is responsible.

We always have a choice in the face of crisis and failure. We can reflect objectively and calmly on what has happened, or we can emote. Emotional arousal can arise from excessive worrying that leads to 'catastrophising'.

Then we may need to take thoughtful stock of the worst and best that may happen to gain a true perspective on our apparent 'catastrophe'.

ACTIVITY/REFLECTION
Reflect on the chart 'Renewing the mind' in Appendix 4 in more detail, applying it to your own situation.

SELF-ESTEEM – THE BEHAVIOURAL SELF
When we have low self-esteem we can very easily slip into behaviour that demonstrates self-sabotage. We self-sabotage opportunities and relationships unknowingly, or even knowingly, reinforcing our low self-esteem: 'I am unlovable therefore I will destroy relationships – so proving what I believe about myself.'

It's like posting something into the pillar box we mentioned earlier. 'This fits the box, I'll put it in.' We link our thought patterns and our behaviour unconsciously: 'I'm a failure, therefore I will sabotage opportunities to be successful so proving what I believe about myself.' Or, 'I'm bad, therefore I will destroy anything good in my life so proving what I believe about myself.'

We need to become our own internal spy, making a note of the times when we recognise ourselves thinking and acting against our own rules and values and working against our own interests.

Lucy found it difficult to make friends in her new workplace. She felt that everyone was part of a group and she didn't like to interrupt the chatting lunchtime gatherings. She thought that she wouldn't be wanted as she was new, so turned down frequent social invitations. Because she felt unwanted, she tended to keep to herself in the office and began to think that people were talking about her. 'They certainly don't talk *to* me,' she reflected.

At her first appraisal her work was praised, but her manager commented that Lucy was considered rather aloof and unfriendly by her colleagues, who had tried to involve her in office social events, but that she seemed to want to sit and work alone and did not join in with their lunchtime conversations.

Lucy realised that she had been assuming that she wasn't wanted as part of the group, partly because she hadn't had the confidence to try to join it. Yet her shyness and uncertainty had been misinterpreted as unfriendliness, resulting in a neutral or negative response from the rest of the office group.

As a result, Lucy had begun listening to a downward pull of negative thoughts and assumptions that had worked against her own best interests, sabotaging her opportunities to become a valued member of the office social group, as well as the workforce.

To break the habit of self-sabotage we need to list those areas in which our internal spy has noticed the habit, and work on each one. (See the activity below.)

For example, if we are habitually late we are wasting not only our own time, but somebody else's. We give the impression that we are disorganised, that the project or person we are late for doesn't matter, and we put ourselves in a position of stress, guilt and unpreparedness.

So, we could begin by telling ourselves that we value ourselves and the other person/project enough to say: 'I cannot always be late' and aim to be no more than five minutes late instead of our usual half hour. In that way we start bridging the gap so that our behaviour starts to improve in small steps.

It's helpful, too, to associate with people who are very supportive. Often, people with low self-esteem have gathered other people with low self-esteem around them, a self-fulfilling prophecy in itself! But if we can choose which of our relationships are constructive, positive and supportive, and give energy and time to developing those relationships further, we will have external support. It's important to spend time with those who support and encourage us, rather than those who keep knocking us down – even in order to raise their own self-esteem.

ACTIVITY/REFLECTION
Ask yourself:

What kind of behaviour do I exhibit which might be sabotaging relationships and opportunities?

How does this fit my belief about myself?

How does this behaviour work against my own interests?

Use the list below to help you identify behaviours that you might have dismissed as unimportant.

How do you behave?
- overwork
- miss lunch breaks
- talk too quickly or too much
- allow others to start up or dominate conversations
- always putting forward the negative possibilities
- always late
- procrastinate
- avoid difficult and irritating people
- can't be bothered to go out, be sociable and have fun
- slip into 'wallflower' mode when with people
- never clear up untidiness and mess
- compulsive cleaning and tidying which is unnecessary
- no time in the diary for 'me' (I am not important)

What actions can you take to stop sabotaging your own best interests?

Who is 'good for you'? How can you nurture that friendship?

SELF-ESTEEM - THE PHYSICAL SELF

If we perceive our bodies as ugly or unattractive, we will consciously or unconsciously alter our behaviour accordingly. We will cringe when someone mentions our name or makes a personal comment; we will avoid eye contact or dress dowdily. All in all we will create a dull, boring impression and in doing so will automatically set ourselves up for rejection.

People often believe that their bodies are essentially bad. Their belief may stem from a misconceived comment, taunts about weight or prominent features, or because of what was communicated by parents or family as they grew up. Sex may have been taboo.

We need to understand our own perception of our physical selves and compare that perception with the understanding that we are made in God's image. Consequently our bodies cannot be 'bad'. We are 'fearfully and wonderfully made …' (Psa. 139:14).

Sex has been given to us as a gift to enjoy; our health and strength are to be a delight to us. God has given us the blessing of food which fuels and supports our bodies, and exercise to strengthen it and to flood our bodies with endomorphs that give us a sense of the 'feel-good factor'.

However, each of our physical gifts is vulnerable to weakness and abuse.

Some with low self-esteem will develop a loathing of their bodies that may lead to under-exercise, over-exercise, eating disorders and self-harming. They lose a sense of self-respect and balance and punish their bodies, and so themselves, for not being 'good enough'.

Jenny grew up believing that she was fat. Her mother had suffered anorexia in her teens and had transmitted a difficult relationship with food to her daughter. Jenny would dress in dark and baggy clothing to hide what she thought was a fat and ugly body. Although she did eat meals, she was preoccupied with their contents and rarely enjoyed her food.

Jenny transferred to a college of further education to study for an Art foundation course and met Jack who was studying catering. Jack was a gifted chef with a lively personality and love of life. He made Jenny laugh, told her she was beautiful and was the first to challenge her wrong beliefs about herself.

He asked how someone with artistic gifts could so avoid colourful clothes, and encouraged her to wear bright colours. Jenny found the changes lifted her mood and gave her confidence simply because others commented on how good she looked.

Her confidence grew as Jack introduced her to the creative side of cookery and re-educated her attitude to food. Jenny's positive experience in a new environment, devoid of negative messages and with people who valued her, helped to break the downward spiral of self-loathing she had become caught in.

God's plan was always that our whole beings should praise Him – and that includes our bodies and all we do with them. Our bodies are the temple of the Holy Spirit. We are God's workmanship and in His eyes we are beautiful.

Our response should be to care for and respect our bodies, making the most of their potential by choosing a healthy diet, taking exercise, allowing space for rest and welcoming times of fun and laughter.

ACTIVITY/REFLECTION
Ask yourself:

Have I ever disregarded my body because I perceive it merely as an unimportant outer case to house the all-important soul?

Do I acknowledge that I am beautiful – an example of God's most exquisite workmanship?

Do I take responsibility for balancing time spent on my own
• Physical exercise
• Rest and relaxation
• Healthy diet
• Fun time
• Appearance?

SELF-ESTEEM - THE EMOTIONAL SELF
Our self-esteem will increase as we learn to manage uncomfortable and overwhelming feelings, rather than let the uncomfortable feelings manage us.

The difficulty is that many of us, particularly as Christians, let our emotions run riot because 'I shouldn't feel this way'; 'I can't be honest with myself. And if I can't be honest with myself, I can't be honest with God. So how can I be honest with anyone else?'

It's important that we get in touch with our feelings and help others to do the same; to label feelings and link them to a source – to what it was that happened to trigger those feelings.

We can follow a 'process' in order to make sense of those overwhelming feelings.

1. We uncover the feeling: 'It's there. Don't hide it.'
2. We identify the feeling: 'It's anger.'
3. We accept the feeling: 'I'm feeling angry about my situation.'
4. We give the feeling some meaning: 'I am feeling angry because I am assuming that I was overlooked and disregarded.'

We can then take our feelings apart and decide what we need to do in response to them – perhaps with the help of a trusted friend or counsellor. In doing so, we control them – we don't allow them to control us.

Selwyn Hughes said, 'all emotions are buried alive'. They are not buried dead, they do not lie dormant. If we have buried guilt or the pain of rejection and have never really accessed it or 'processed' it, it will fester and even grow internally.

It will, inevitably, manifest itself in some way. That might be depression, stress or a physical illness.

Low self-esteem often means that we allow our emotions to push us around, rather than put them in their 'processed' place.

Maria had been asked to help to organise the recording of team scores at her son's sports day. She was keen to get involved because she had always felt too nervous to do anything before, and her son Sam felt left out when his friends' mums were involved.

On the day, Maria got herself ready in good time and drove to the school playing fields. She found it difficult to park and, as she circled the ground, became increasingly stressed. She began to tell herself that this was typical, and that she would probably do a bad job anyway. Becoming angrier with herself for not being able to park, and cross at the school for expecting her to help, she decided that perhaps it would be better if she didn't go. They could find someone else – somebody else would do it better anyway. She would only embarrass Sam, turning up so angry and cross. So, driving past a perfectly acceptable space, Maria went home. Arriving home she felt much better and convinced herself that it was all for the best, she couldn't have done it well anyway – until she saw the disappointed and hurt expression on her son's face.

Maria had allowed her lack of self-confidence to heighten her stress levels, send her negative commentaries and control her actions to such an extent that the stress and low self-confidence had been allowed to manage her: to her great regret and her son's.

ACTIVITY/REFLECTION

Look at the process we might adopt to deal with overwhelming feelings (above).

How might we remind ourselves to make this process a positive habit?

Keep a journal or notebook of your progress and use it prayerfully.

SELF-ESTEEM - THE SPIRITUAL SELF

Healthy self-esteem means that we don't have to hide from God, from other people, or from ourselves. Jennifer Minney summarises it as 'the confidence to approach God just as we are, perfectly assured of our welcome at all times. This in turn leads to the confidence to face the world.'[2]

Healthy self-esteem depends on our knowledge of God's perception of us. For Christians, self-esteem is the assurance of being of value to God.

It is based on God's perception of us as essentially good, valuable, approved, lovable and loved and leads to a realistic view of ourselves and others. We don't expect too much or too little and are thus able to form good relationships.

John felt sure that God was calling him into the ministry. But he called back!

'Lord,' he said, 'I know You are asking me to do this, but I am not gifted. I do not have the ability to do well. I am not the man these people need. There are so many gifted church leaders out there. I can't be one of them.'

John was challenged by an elder in his church who asked him why he wasn't being obedient. 'Do you not think God knows who He needs to do His work? Have you forgotten that He equips who He sends? Do you doubt God's judgment on these issues?' John was helped to understand that God's image of us is very different to our own; that even though God sees as us as we really are, He also sees the way in which we are being changed to be more like Jesus. He sees the potential, He sees our heart and He knows what He can do through us. John had to learn to listen to God's messages about his worth and potential, not the self-doubt and 'put downs' his own internal messages were sending.

It's important, too, that we take seriously Jesus' commandment to love your neighbour as you love yourself. As Christians we so often say that we love our neighbour but we don't finish the command. We say, 'I love them and I will do everything for them, but I won't love me.' It's important that we learn to love ourselves simply because God loves us.

ACTIVITY/REFLECTION
Ask yourself:

Do I love my neighbour as I love myself?

- How patient am I with myself?
- How kind am I to myself?
- How angry do I get with myself?
- Do I protect myself?
- How easy do I find it to trust myself?
- Do I value myself as God values me?

God gives us great worth. Each one of us is precious and unique in His sight, like a pearl or rare stone. We are the apple of His eye. We have the assurance of being accepted and approved by God. That knowledge should line everything we say and feel about ourselves with pure gold. It should be the clarion call message to silence all other negative messages: 'I am loved by God, the Creator of the universe, the heavenly Father, the Lord of all.'

ACTIVITY

Take some time to dwell positively on who you are in God's sight. Pray as you do so, and do not allow any negative thoughts to challenge your prayerful God-given estimate of the uniqueness of you.

Copy the following into your notebook or journal or write it out and pin it up somewhere where just you can be reminded of what it means.

WHAT I LIKE ABOUT MYSELF

I am good at ... (eg cookery, listening)

I help others by ... (befriending, shopping, caring for children)

I enjoy a good relationship with ...

What I have learned to do for myself (eg computer skills, new job, using a drill)

Fears I have overcome (shyness, flying, speaking in public)

I have survived (illness, bereavement, divorce, disability, redundancy)

I have tried new interests/places/food/skills

I enjoy ... (having fun, seeing friends, completing a task)

One way in which I have grown as a person is:

Support I have been able to ask for is:

Other things I am proud of:

I am proud of being me, because I am wonderfully and uniquely made by God, different to anyone else, and I have my own strengths.

Signed: _____ Date: _____

REFLECTION

YOU ARE VERY SPECIAL

In all the world there is nobody, nobody like you.
Since the beginning of time there has never been
another person like you. Nobody has your smile,
your eyes, your hands, your hair.
Nobody owns your handwriting, your voice.
YOU'RE SPECIAL.

You're different from any other person who lived in the
history of the universe. You are the only one in the
whole creation who has your particular set of abilities.

There is always someone who is better at one thing or another. But nobody in the universe can reach the quality of the combination of your talents, your feelings.

Like a roomful of musical instruments, some might excel in one way or another, but nobody can match the symphonic sound when all are played together. YOUR SYMPHONY.

Nobody can paint your brush strokes. Nobody has your taste for food or music or dance or art. Nobody in the universe sees things as you do. In all time there has never been anyone who laughs in exactly your way, and what makes you laugh, or cry, or think may have a totally different response in another. SO ... YOU'RE SPECIAL.

Through all eternity no one will ever walk, talk, think or do exactly like you. YOU'RE SPECIAL. You're rare and in all rarity there is enormous value and because of your value the need for you to imitate anyone else is absolutely wrong. Please realise that God made you for a special purpose. He has a job for you to do that nobody else can do as well as you can. Out of the billions of applicants one is qualified. Only one has the unique and right combination of what it takes and that one is YOU.

You are very special

(19th century Anon – revised EJB March 1982)

PRAYER

Father God,

As I have read these pages, You have shown me afresh just how special I am to You. You value each of the unique details about me and rejoice in them. I am worth so much that You sacrificed Your own Son in order to know relationship with me. You gave Your all for my all. Nothing in my past, my present or the unknown future can change this fact: I am Yours and You are mine. I am *that* important to You: loved; precious; delightful.

Thank You, Lord.

Amen.

A FAMILIAR STORY

Finally, a wonderful story about a woman with low self-esteem whose life was turned around because of one simple meeting on a very ordinary day. I have called her Kazia. Kazia's story is true and there is safety in the telling, as Kazia's story is very much in the public domain.

Kazia's childhood was not a healthy and encouraging one. As she grew, her sense of self-esteem was so low that she became desperate for the love and approval that her parents could not give. Her family life was dysfunctional and her relationship with her dad wasn't close. He often told her that she was no good; he never said, 'I love you.' Her mother was a weak and saddened woman, worn down by the demands of marriage and children. She had little left to give to Kazia.

Kazia felt she didn't belong. In fact she felt a complete misfit in life and deep down she believed that there really was something wrong with her. Her inner voice often called her 'unlovable'. Guilty and ashamed of who she was, life was tough.

As she grew into a beautiful young woman, Kazia discovered that the only way she knew how to feel valued was to give herself to men. At least this sent her the message that she was worth something, even if that message seemed somehow contradictory and often left her feeling empty and used.

Her promiscuous and lonely lifestyle meant that by the time she was in her late thirties she had lived with five husbands and was desperate to keep her live-in partner. And she was lonely.

She felt so ashamed of her life that she couldn't face her peers. Kazia didn't join in with the usual social rounds, the birthday parties, the chats in the school yard, the laughter she heard from the groups of mothers as they watched their children play. She couldn't be part of their group or do the things they did.

So she ended up living an isolated and lonely life, a very needy woman, her low self-esteem affecting the way she lived, taking away her hope.

One ordinary day, Kazia's life changed.

Just as her self-esteem had hit rock bottom and she wondered how much longer she could go on, she met a man. He wasn't like the other men she had met. Yes, she knew she had said that to herself so many times. But this man really *was* different. He loved her. Most of the other men in her life had loved her in their own way, but their love wasn't enough for her. It was self-seeking, imperfect.

This man was from a completely different culture. In fact, racial hatred separated Kazia's culture from His. His culture and custom dictated that He should not even speak to a woman – let alone a woman from her part of the country – but He crossed the cultural barriers and spoke to Kazia.

It was a hot afternoon. The kind of afternoon where the dust seems dustier than it has ever been and the glare of the sun plays tricks, pooling water on the ground ahead and making you long for springs of fresh water. That was the draw, really; both of them were thirsty, but in very different ways.

As Kazia was going about her business the man, sitting on a wall nearby, asked Kazia for a drink of water.

She swung around to see Him there, staring at her. She was used to men looking at her, but not like this. Not with such openness and honesty. She was intrigued. But her defensiveness flared up and before she could stop herself she snapped at Him. 'I'm not part of Your culture, You must be out of Your mind to speak to me … are You sick or something?' She realised that, as ever, in her prickly state of battered self, she was picking a fight.

But He did not respond. He simply held up a bottle and said something quite extraordinary: 'Everyone who drinks this water will be thirsty again, but whoever drinks the water I give him will never thirst.'

'He *is* mad,' she thought, planning an escape route and turning to walk away.

But He continued: 'Indeed, the water I give him will become in him a spring of water welling up to eternal life.'

She stopped in her tracks, stunned. What did He mean? If you drink water I give, then you will never thirst again. He had asked Kazia for a drink. Yet now He was offering her a drink that meant she would never feel thirsty, never feel needy. And it would give her *life*?

Kazia was intrigued. Mad or not, she recognised that this man had exposed her need to receive something far deeper than just water.

She turned and watched Him. He smiled.

'Go and call your husband,' He said.

Kazia replied, 'I have no husband,' all the time wondering, 'Perhaps He knows why I'm here by myself in the middle of the day. Maybe someone has told Him about the rumours, most of which are true. Perhaps He knows I have no husband. That I have had five, but that the man I am with …'

She drew closer, then as gently as a doctor unwraps a wound to examine it, this man took the cover off her life. The wounds were deep. Past hurts, past disappointments. There were many open wounds and one which wept, even as she wept, quietly, at His tenderness, His knowledge, His unspoken understanding. Kazia realised that He knew that she was living with a man whose love could not embrace her neediness to feel valued. Somehow, deep within her very being, beyond the hurt and pain, she knew that this man could do that … this man's love was different. He was more than the love of her life. He *was* love. He *was* life – and she wanted to drink.

As Kazia continued to talk to this man, she realised with sudden, deep conviction that He was the Messiah, God's Son, Jesus. This man Jesus totally accepted her. He accepted her despite her wounds, even *because* of them, and gave her an assurance, a certainty of feeling valued for the first time in her life.

It didn't matter what she had done in the past. It didn't matter that she hadn't been loved by her parents. It didn't matter that she'd had five husbands and counting. Because now she mattered to someone who esteemed her for being a woman; for being herself. For the first time, Kazia felt valued by a man because of who she was, not because she had given her body to him for sex.

In finding herself accepted, Kazia was able to accept herself for the first time in her life. It felt good to be her. In that short time with Jesus, she experienced a new freedom, a joy in life. So much so that she ran back to her home, to the women watching their children play, to the mothers in the school yard, and she said, 'Come and see! Come and meet a man who told me all the things I ever did, and still accepts me.'

They followed – they had to; her joy and faith were infectious. They had never seen her like this before. She was no longer cowering in shame, hiding from their glances, avoiding their company. She was free.

So they went with her to meet Jesus.

Kazia was never the same again. She felt valued, loved, held in high esteem, by the man who asked her for a drink – and who by doing so, had given her life.

(Based on the story of the Samaritan Woman, John 4:1–42)

APPENDIX 1:

A SELF-ESTEEM SCALE

Read the statements below and put a mark next to each question in the column that best reflects how you feel about yourself. Try to be honest about how you see yourself … there is no right or wrong answer.

Statements	Yes, definitely	Yes, mostly	Yes, occasionally	No, not at all
1. I value and appreciate myself				
2. I like myself				
3. I often think of myself as a failure				
4. I feel that I have good qualities				
5. I am kind to myself and look after myself				
6. I think other people are better than me				
7. I am always self-critical				
8. I respect myself				
9. I am worthless				
10. I feel I don't have much to be proud of				
11. I enjoy participating in life				
12. I often feel inadequate				

To score give a value to each of the 12 statements as follows;
- For statements: **1, 2, 4, 5, 8, 11**
  Yes, definitely = 3   Yes, mostly = 2   Yes, occasionally = 1   No, not all = 0

- For statements: **3, 6, 7, 9, 10, 12**
  Yes, definitely = 0   Yes, mostly = 1   Yes, occasionally = 2   No, not all = 3

MY SCORE IS _____ THIS MEANS:

31-36 = very healthy self-esteem
24-30 = fairly healthy self-esteem
17-23 = middling self-esteem
10-16 = low self-esteem
1-9 = very low self-esteem

APPENDIX 2:

QUESTIONNAIRE TO ASSESS YOUR SELF-ESTEEM

Answer each question by writing a number in the box provided.
Grade yourself 1-5 as follows;

1 = No, definitely not
2 = No, not really
3 = Sometimes/maybe/some aspects
4 = Yes, a little
5 = Yes, definitely

The Thinking Self

Do you believe that you generally perceive others accurately?

Do you believe that you generally perceive yourself accurately?

Are you able to rejoice when others achieve?

Have you the confidence to risk trying new things?

The Behavioural Self

Are you able to form close relationships?

Are you able to meet deadlines?

Are you able to give yourself time in the diary for your needs?

Can you accept practical help from others?

The Physical Self

☐ Are you comfortable with your body?

☐ Do you look after your body?

☐ Are you able to enjoy sex?

☐ Are you able to receive compliments about your appearance?

The Emotional Self

☐ Are you able to express feelings and show affection?

☐ Are you able to accept love and affection from others?

☐ Are you able to accept your weaknesses?

☐ Are you able to feel confident about who you are, without others' approval?

The Spiritual Self

☐ Are you able to appreciate beauty?

☐ Are you able to relate to God as a loving Father?

☐ Are you able to trust God?

☐ Can you accept that God loves you unconditionally?

☐ **TOTAL SCORE**

Total your score (marking your score out of 100). The higher the score the healthier your self-esteem.

APPENDIX 3:

THE LOW SELF-ESTEEM CYCLE

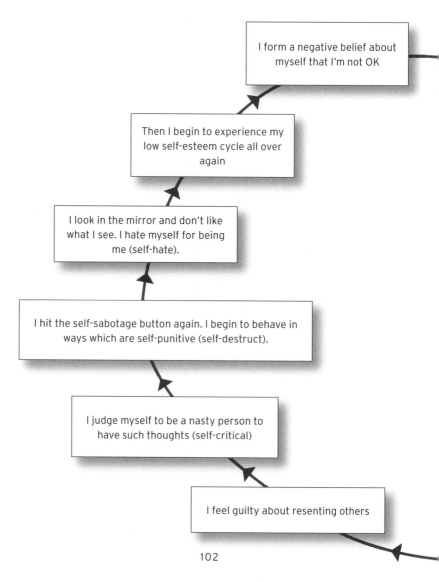

I form a negative belief about myself that I'm not OK

Then I begin to experience my low self-esteem cycle all over again

I look in the mirror and don't like what I see. I hate myself for being me (self-hate).

I hit the self-sabotage button again. I begin to behave in ways which are self-punitive (self-destruct).

I judge myself to be a nasty person to have such thoughts (self-critical)

I feel guilty about resenting others

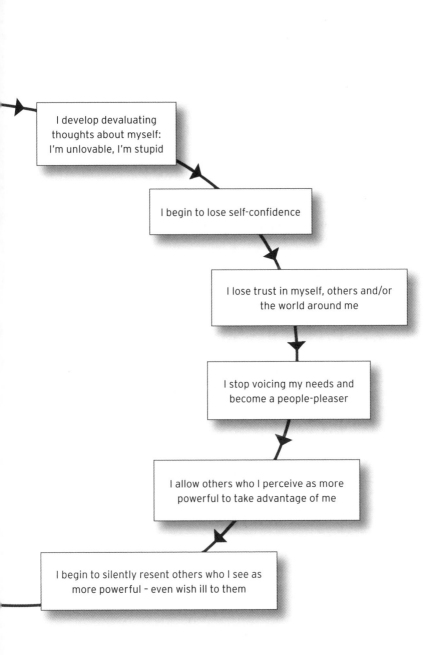

APPENDIX 4:

RENEWING THE MIND

Romans 12:2

Be transformed by the renewing of your mind:
1. Identify and acknowledge negative thoughts attached to uncomfortable emotions.
2. Choose to challenge the untrue thoughts.
3. Choose to agree with the Word of God and His perception of you.

Identify the uncomfortable emotion	I choose to disagree with the old negative thoughts	I choose to agree with the new thoughts based on truth	New emotion
Guilt	It's all my fault	I am not to blame for everything. If it's my fault, I will confess my sin and Jesus will forgive me. 1 John 1:9; Romans 8:1	Freedom and forgiveness
Rejection	No one wants me	Jesus wants me, He chose and accepted me. I am part of His family. Isaiah 41:9; 1 Corinthians 12:13	Love and acceptance
Rejection and need for attention	I have to work harder to be noticed and accepted	Jesus sees all that I do and says 'Well done' Matthew 25:21	Acceptance and approval
Worthlessness	I am nothing and I don't belong	I am precious to God because He chose me, and delights in me. Isaiah 43:4; Psalm 139:1; Ephesians 1:11-12	Worth
Worthlessness	What I do is not good enough	God accepts me as I am. I don't have to prove myself. John 1:12; 1 John 3:1; James 2:5	Worth from 'being' not 'doing'
Fear	I am frightened, I will fail	I will do my best and His grace will be sufficient for me. Isaiah 41:10; 2 Corinthians 12:9	Confidence

NOTES

CHAPTER 1
1. www.wiktionary.org
2. Joanna and Alister McGrath, *The Dilemma of Self-Esteem* (Leicester: Crossway Books, 1992), p.29.
3. Sue Atkinson, *Building Self-Esteem* (Oxford: Lion, 2001), p.104.
4. Jennifer Minney, *Self-Esteem, The Way of Humility* (Yeovil: Silvertree Publishing, 2000).
5. Steve Chalke, *One God* (Spring Harvest Study Guide, 2006), p.28.

CHAPTER 2
1. Barrie Wade, 'Truth', in his book of poems, *Conkers* (Oxford: Oxford University Press, 1989). Used by permission.

CHAPTER 3
1. D. Seamands, *Healing for Damaged Emotions* (Amersham-on-the-Hill: Scripture Press Foundation [UK] Ltd, 1986), p.101.
2. www.quotationspage.com/quotes/Anais_Nin/
3. D. Seamands, op. cit., p.15.
4. Nigel Hemming, *Beautiful God*, from *Come, Now is the Time*, Vineyard Music, 1998. Used with permission.

CHAPTER 4
1. As quoted in J.C. Arnold, *The Lost Art of Forgiving* (Farmington, PA: Plough Publishing House, 1998).
2. Jennifer Minney, *Self-Esteem, The Way of Humility* (Yeovil: Silvertree Publishing, 2000), p.16.

National Distributors

UK: (and countries not listed below)
CWR, Waverley Abbey House, Waverley Lane, Farnham, Surrey GU9 8EP.
Tel: (01252) 784700 Outside UK (+44) 1252 784700

AUSTRALIA: CMC Australasia, PO Box 519, Belmont, Victoria 3216.
Tel: (03) 5241 3288 Fax: (03) 5241 3290

CANADA: Cook Communications Ministries, PO Box 98, 55 Woodslee Avenue, Paris, Ontario N3L 3E5.
Tel: 1800 263 2664

GHANA: Challenge Enterprises of Ghana, PO Box 5723, Accra.
Tel: (021) 222437/223249 Fax: (021) 226227

HONG KONG: Cross Communications Ltd, 1/F, 562A Nathan Road, Kowloon.
Tel: 2780 1188 Fax: 2770 6229

INDIA: Crystal Communications, 10-3-18/4/1, East Marredpalli, Secunderabad – 500026,
Andhra Pradesh.
Tel/Fax: (040) 27737145

KENYA: Keswick Books and Gifts Ltd, PO Box 10242, Nairobi.
Tel: (02) 331692/226047 Fax: (02) 728557

MALAYSIA: Salvation Book Centre (M) Sdn Bhd, 23 Jalan SS 2/64, 47300 Petaling Jaya, Selangor.
Tel: (03) 78766411/78766797 Fax: (03) 78757066/78756360

NEW ZEALAND: CMC Australasia, PO Box 36015, Lower Hutt.
Tel: 0800 449 408 Fax: 0800 449 049

NIGERIA: FBFM, Helen Baugh House, 96 St Finbarr's College Road, Akoka, Lagos.
Tel: (01) 7747429/4700218/825775/827264

PHILIPPINES: OMF Literature Inc, 776 Boni Avenue, Mandaluyong City.
Tel: (02) 531 2183 Fax: (02) 531 1960

SINGAPORE: Armour Publishing Pte Ltd, Block 203A Henderson Road,
11–06 Henderson Industrial Park, Singapore 159546.
Tel: 6 276 9976 Fax: 6 276 7564

SOUTH AFRICA: Struik Christian Books, 80 MacKenzie Street, PO Box 1144, Cape Town 8000.
Tel: (021) 462 4360 Fax: (021) 461 3612

SRI LANKA: Christombu Publications (Pvt) Ltd., Bartleet House, 65 Braybrooke Place,
Colombo 2. Tel: (9411) 2421073/2447665

TANZANIA: CLC Christian Book Centre, PO Box 1384, Mkwepu Street, Dar es Salaam.
Tel/Fax: (022) 2119439

USA: Cook Communications Ministries, PO Box 98, 55 Woodslee Avenue, Paris, Ontario N3L 3E5,
Canada.
Tel: 1800 263 2664

ZIMBABWE: Word of Life Books (Pvt) Ltd, Christian Media Centre, 8 Aberdeen Road, Avondale,
PO Box A480 Avondale, Harare.
Tel: (04) 333355 or 091301188

For email addresses, visit the CWR website: www.cwr.org.uk

CWR is a registered charity – Number 294387

CWR is a limited company registered in England – Registration Number 1990308

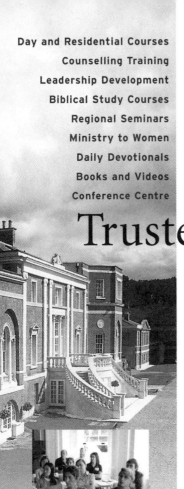

Day and Residential Courses
Counselling Training
Leadership Development
Biblical Study Courses
Regional Seminars
Ministry to Women
Daily Devotionals
Books and Videos
Conference Centre

Trusted all Over the World

CWR HAS GAINED A WORLDWIDE reputation as a centre of excellence for Bible-based training and resources. From our headquarters at Waverley Abbey House, Farnham, England, we have been serving God's people for 40 years with a vision to help apply God's Word to everyday life and relationships. The daily devotional *Every Day with Jesus* is read by nearly a million readers an issue in more than 150 countries, and our unique courses in biblical studies and pastoral care are respected all over the world. Waverley Abbey House provides a conference centre in a tranquil setting.

For free brochures on our seminars and courses, conference facilities, or a catalogue of CWR resources, please contact us at the following address.
CWR, Waverley Abbey House, Waverley Lane, Farnham, Surrey GU9 8EP, UK

Telephone: +44 (0)1252 784700
Email: mail@cwr.org.uk
Website: www.cwr.org.uk

 Applying God's Word
to everyday life and relationships

Other titles available in the Waverley Abbey Insight Series

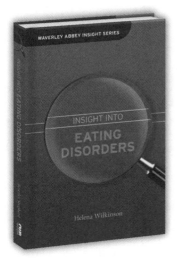

Insight into Eating Disorders
Helena Wilkinson

An eating disorder is like an iceberg, with the visible tip of symptoms dwarfed by the pain below the surface. Helena Wilkinson, who herself suffered from anorexia as a teenager, examines this complex subject – and gives help in thawing out the iceberg.

ISBN-13: 978-1-85345-410-3
ISBN-10: 1-85345-410-9
£7.50 (plus p&p)

Insight into Stress
Beverley Shepherd

An examination of the basics of stress, this book provides practical help and advice on this complex subject. Topics covered include how stress arises, recognising warning signs and coping with the demands and expectations of ourselves and others.

ISBN-13: 978-1-85345-384-7
ISBN-10: 1-85345-384-6
£7.50 (plus p&p)

Insight into Bereavement
Wendy Bray & Diana Priest

Bereavements follow a similar path of loss, disbelief, grief and adaptation. This book provides sound advice on coping, whether the bereavement is of a loved one, a marriage or a livelihood. It looks at the effects of loss and at being a channel of God's love to the bereaved.

ISBN-13: 978-1-85345-385-4
ISBN-10: 1-85345-385-4
£7.50 (plus p&p)